CHASING
FISH TALES

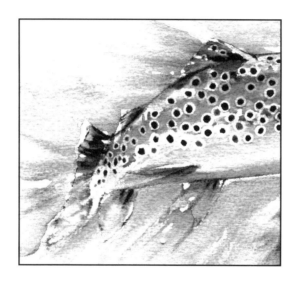

CHASING
FISH TALES

A Freewheeling Year in the Life of an Angler

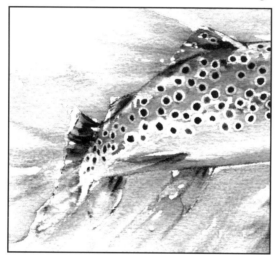

JOHN HOLT

Illustrations by
Jenifer Thomas

COUNTRYSPORT PRESS
Traverse City, Michigan

First Edition
10 9 8 7 6 5 4 3 2 1

Published by Countrysport Press
P.O. Box 1856, Traverse City, MI 49685

Book and jacket design - Saxon Design, Cedar, Michigan

Printed in the United States of America

ISBN 0-924357-36-3   Trade Edition
ISBN 0-924357-37-1 Deluxe Limited Edition

For Tony Acerrano

W̲ithout determined support and encouragement from Michael McIntosh, this book would not exist. I also want to extend my sincere thanks to Doug Truax for all of his help as well as to Bryan Bilinski and Lon Deckard. The Club Car is open. The author gratefully acknowledges permission to reprint an excerpt from "The Wer-Trout" contained in the short story collection *Heart Songs* by E. Annie Proulx, © 1988.

CONTENTS

Winter
IN THE FRIGID BEGINNING

Fly casting on the ice restores sanity. Early season on the Bitterroot. Remembrances of Morocco. Carp fillets at the bottom of the Grand Canyon. Skwala stoneflies.

Spring
THE GAME HEATS UP

Toothy pike on a fly. Float tubing for big rainbows. Hunting trout east of the mountains. Floating the Bighorn. The wicked chutes of the Madison. A Video Screenplay from Hell. On the Smith River. Braving the wind for big trout on the Blackfeet Reservation.

Summer
THE FEVER BURNS WHITE HOT

Browns and char at the base of Iceland's glacier. In Montana's high country for goldens and a brush with death. Searching for the elusive bull trout. Running with the grizzlies. Westslope and Yellowstone cutthroats.

Fall
THE SWEET SEASON APPROACHES

Savoring the uncrowded streams of autumn. Spawning brookies, big browns on the feed. Large lake trout provide unusual sport. All's right with the world.

WINTER

IN THE
FRIGID
BEGINNING

IN THE
FRIGID
BEGINNING

A thick cloud of fog rolls in and the chill rips right through the layers of warm clothing down deep into my bones. The forested shoreline, not more than one hundred feet away, is out of sight. There is absolutely no sound. No wind. Nothing.

Staring at a little round hole bored through the thick ice is ridiculous. This is sport? Others may think so, but I no longer want to be counted among their disturbed number. All I can see is dark water. There are no trout and my line is hanging limply in the water with ice crystals forming here and there. But just being outside is good, if only because this frozen activity is at least not as futile as standing around looking out the frosted windows of my living room. As the days lengthen appreciably I know my chances of surviving another winter get better. Maybe massive doses of Stelazine coupled with wet sheets and restraints will not be needed this winter. I tell myself, "You can do it, Boy. Spring is coming. Hang in there."

I finish off the last of the brandied hot chocolate in the metal Thermos, reel in the line, toss the rig into the mist, and grab the axe. Sure, I'll make it through winter and live to dance in the warm light of spring, but I need to fly fish, not ice fish, NOW. The hell with the icy miasma and the temperature that is flirting obscenely with the zero-degree mark. Fly fishing. That's what I crave—to feel the flex of the rod as it loads on the back cast and to watch the line unfurl in a rush ahead of me.

The cold, sharp metal of the blade strikes the ice with a crisp clanging that dies swiftly in the fog. Shards of ice explode into the air, nicking me. Thin lines of blood run down my face and drip onto the small pile of shattered lake at my feet. I strike again, ripping deeper into the lake's hard surface. And then again and again.

I'm way out of it now. The blade rises and falls over and over, whacking away. Minutes pass. I shed my waxed cotton coat, then a sweater and finally a wool shirt. I roll up the sleeves on my long underwear. Sweat runs down my face. More time disappears and a lengthening tear some twenty, maybe thirty feet long by six wide takes form in the middle of this frozen, misty madness. Dark, blue-green water and slush slops onto the ice and under my insulated boots. The footing is greasy on the ice. The cold stabs my toes and I continue to hack away wildly, elongating and widening the wound in the lake.

The gash is over fifty feet long now. The fog is getting thicker and I can't see the end of it. Skirting the edge of my miniature man-made lake, I swing at random pieces of ice, mini-icebergs, drifting in my little ocean. They steam away from me like translucent barges.

The black metal of my fly rod case is covered in rime and snow. The suede reel case is soaked and partially frozen. Probably no sane person would have brought this gear on an ice fishing outing to begin with. But who's sane in Montana during the winter? My hands are hot from the exertion of smacking the lake. They glow red in the gloom. I attach the reel to the beautifully made graphite rod, string the line through the guides, and then tie a #20 Blue-Winged Olive to the 7X tippet. Perhaps not the perfect pattern for fishing amidst ice floes, but then selection is not important right now.

I strip line from the reel which screeches across the emptiness of the lake. More and more of the bright yellow line whistles back and forth over the still lake. I lose sight of the end of the line as it unfurls on the back cast. Then I shoot it out over my rectangular sea and watch as it settles softly through the air onto the smooth surface already starting to freeze.

Everything turns dead still. A raven croaks overhead, invisible. I hear the flapping of its wings and the air rushing past its black feathers, but I never spot the bird.

I wait but nothing happens. No brightly speckled brook trout rises to the fly and I reach back to cast again but am stopped, quickly and powerfully. The line has frozen into the water. My lake is turning solid again. The few minutes of casting were a glorious reminder of what I love to do as much as anything in the world: to work a line over a river or the mirrored surface of a lake filled with wild, colorful trout. It requires intense concentration to mend and correct the line as it drifts through the prime holding water. The slightest drag caused by the shifting, flickering surface currents can expose my efforts as a fraud and the fish will not move to the fly at the slender end of my leader. Or worse yet, they will be spooked by my clumsiness and inaccuracy, fleeing for cover, and ending their feeding for at least an hour and perhaps the day. Fly fishing, when it works and I am doing it right, creates the illusion of life and nothing less will fool trout, even when the fishing is easy. These creatures may possess diminutive brain pans, but they know a fake when they see one.

There is satisfaction in taking a trout—in seeing it rise through the water and hit the fly, in feeling the natural power as it runs for cover at the first suggestion of resistance from the rod. And there is tremendous satisfaction and wonder when I hold the trout in my hands and marvel at its colorful perfection and strength, and then when I release the fish and watch it swiftly disappear in the depths. Fly fishing is the perfect pursuit for me. The chase, the offer of an artificial that mimics a real food source or preys on some atavistic response, the attention to the fine details of presentation and drift, the playing of a wild fish, and then the release—all of this is as close to godlike as an imperfect human can hope to be, and it is more than enough. Always.

But God! I think I hate winter in Montana. When will this end? February is hell on earth for a fly fisher. Spring is a distant two months away, a chunk of time I may not endure. Time drags, hangs, lingers—making life difficult for a derelict angler. Whiskey never really works. Writing gets stale. Sleeping twenty-two hours a day is grim. Visions of fly fishing on perfect, warm, blue-sky summer days run through my mind with hellish repetition.

This day's fishing is a dead issue and I head back to the truck along an old logging road buried under several feet of snow. My snowshoes sink several inches in the powdery stuff with a gentle "puff." The forest is silent, but special in its winter isolation. How something this cold and apparently barren can be so full of life in only a matter of weeks is a good mystery. There will be wildflowers here by April—glacier lilies, camus, even violets. Birds will chatter among themselves as they stake out nesting territories in the bushes and in the branches overhead. Deer will move quietly through the trees on the thick covering of pine needles. But that is April and this is the dead of a very cold winter. I need a break. A chance to stand in the sun and cast a line in earnest. To catch a fish. Any fish.

I have a little money saved and the bills are paid, almost. I'm going to visit a friend at his warm lodge in the Bitterroot for a few days. Maybe some good will come of this modest attempt at spontaneity. The chance to talk fishing with a friend might take some of the edge off winter. I could even head south to the sun and warmth, cheating on the season. Load up the truck and run for the border, if only for a couple of weeks. That would be enough to tide me over. When I returned, February would be finished and March, at least, holds honest promise of spring. It could work.

"Whoosh!"

A burgundy Saab Turbo zips by me as I toss the tackle in the back of the battered truck. Happy faces are turned in my direction, looking through steamy windows. Their mouths drop open as I leer and brandish the axe. The car speeds up and vanishes around a sharp curve.

Time to get out of Whitefish while I still can. I'll be back later when the trout are closer to life. Tomorrow or the next day it's off to Darby and slight intimations of sanity.

The "Post and Pole" sign comes up on the right. I turn left onto a small, snow-covered tributary of Highway 93 several miles south of Hamilton in the Bitterroot Valley. My friend, John Talia, is here ahead of me. Fresh tire tracks mark the way. The sky is clear, the day cold, but tomorrow is expected to be overcast and warmer. Perhaps a bit of midge action is in the offing. I brought my four-weight just in case.

I look forward to seeing John. We have not fished together since last May on some lakes along the Rocky Mountain Front. Work and convoluted travel schemed to keep us off the water together. Good friends are valuable finds. Those that are easy to get along with on the road for days at a time, who can take the difficult, bizarre, and twisted in stride usually with a shrug of the shoulders and a "here-we-go-again" smile, are a gift from above. John is one of them. We've covered several thousand miles chasing browns, rattlesnakes, turkeys, rainbows, and good food. We've fished from sunup to dark for days on end in the windswept Rockies. And we've floated some damn fine rivers. He's a skilled outdoorsman and can spot a snake slithering among the rocks far better than I. He's a good cook, knows his wine, and is an accomplished fly fisher. The only weakness I've observed is his predilection for plugging a Bob Seger CD into his rig's music system before 7:00 a.m. There was a period in my life, possibly all too brief, when I believed that the proper way to kick off a new day consisted of John driving like hell to some obscure water with "The Fire Inside" raging away through eighteen or so speakers while I sipped a warm Pilsner from an exotic origin, someplace like St. Louis. Suffice it to say that we've known each other for a few seasons now and have fished a little water together.

His Bronco is parked in front of the lodge. Smoke trails from the chimney in the still air. Talia is inside sitting in front of the fire and watching a tape on fly fishing. Awful stuff most of the time, but what can a person do in winter in the Rockies?

"Holt. You made it. There are some midges coming off the river."

"It's twenty degrees outside," I say and pour a glass of wine from a bottle on the kitchen counter.

"I know but there's a window of about forty minutes when the sun's out around two o'clock," Talia offers.

I can see a three-weight rigged in a corner, the barest suggestion of a fly connected to a diminutive tippet. What did I expect? John fishes as hard as anyone I know. If there's a chance for a trout, he'll take it, and I brought my long underwear and neoprene waders. I'm ready.

After a superb dinner of Caesar salad, grilled steak, and baked potatoes, with a glass or two of wine, we're back in front of the fire watching a Warriors-Lakers game off the dish and telling lies about the previous season. Talia got his elk over in the Missouri Breaks in November after a two-week effort and I recount a large brown fooled in Shields River country above Livingston. This goes on for some time, as only those who love good country can appreciate. The air is blue with cigar smoke and several empty wine bottles stand mutely on the marble table before us.

"Talia, we've got to get over to Morocco, there's great brown trout fishing in some spring creeks running out of the Atlas Mountains," I suggest while removing the cork on a bottle of something white. "The country's great. You can live like a king for nothing. No one's out there fishing."

"Maybe they don't want to get killed, Holt. You know the local crowd doesn't care too much for Americans."

"No guts, no glory."

"That's what I'm afraid of."

"Relax. We can do it. When I fished there twenty years ago I was a long-haired hipster. The tourist jive in Europe was garbage. Posturing bozos practicing the Europe-On-Five-Dollars-A-Day game. Pathetic stuff. I flew into the airport outside of Casablanca late at night from Athens. What a flight. No drinks. Hot as hell. A beater prop-jet stuffed to the gills with locals hauling chickens and baskets of stuff I didn't want to know about," I said, topping off our glasses. The fire was burning nicely and the game on TV was in the third quarter. Serious hyperbole was looming on the conversational horizon. Turning to my friend I began ...

I took a taxi into the city. The music on the cab's radio was strange with weird wailings, moanings, and horns sounding like they were in some pain. A bright but not full moon illuminated a landscape of sand, rock, and palm trees. The silhouettes of camels flanked the roadside. Casablanca was quiet but bright this late at night. Neon and arc lights illuminated a city of old and modern styles crammed together in urban juxtaposition. This was a big place but it was not New York or Chicago or L.A. The architecture was downscale Taos and neo-Manila with dingy facades and few buildings over twenty stories. The hotel I was taken to, any would do at this point, was a three-story affair with a single light on over the tall double door. I paid the cabbie for the ride, probably three or four hundred dollars. I was unfamiliar with the money system. Despite the Sahara Desert lying over the Atlas Mountains to the southeast, the ocean exerted a humid influence on the atmosphere. The air was warm and damp. Large moths clattered in and out of the light's glow. The man at the main desk in the tiled foyer smiled, took another five hundred dollars, and called, "Boy, front." Boy? Front? The "boy" also smiled, took my back-pack, and led me to the third floor and a room that featured a bed, dresser, light, and bathroom complete with bidet. Luxury. I tipped the guy about two hundred dollars. He smiled and vanished. A walk-through window gave way to a narrow balcony that revealed the city and the harbor. I pulled out a bottle of duty-free Scotch and drank in the strangeness of the new surroundings. Distant sounds of ships and buoys hooting out on the water drifted on the night breeze. But the city was calm and the time was just 2:00 a.m. Where was the nightlife, the chaotic madness of reveling drunks, and the speeding cars and trucks? This was a different sort of town. I could already tell that this place beat the hell out of Europe and its homogenized wonders.

In the morning, after a sound but brief sleep, I hauled my bags downstairs and hailed a cab to the bus station which resembled Boston's North Station, Arab style. I drank some very sweet tea, bought a ticket to Agadir, 350 miles south down the coast of the Atlantic, for perhaps a thousand dollars, and climbed on a bus that resembled the archaic yellow machines of my school days. It was packed with Muslims dressed in robes and turbans. There were chickens and two goats. More live creatures in cages were tied to the rack above. A sweet smell filled the bus before we started. I was seated on the back bench seat but could see the driver and his assistant firing up a pipe with what must have been the famous Moroccan zero-zero hash-hish. After the flight's crew was properly prepared, we pulled out and wound our way along a two-lane highway, first through almost junglelike growth, then camel and palm studded sands before climbing slowly up along a broad, rocky bench overlooking the ocean. A perpetual din of stoned adult babble, screaming children, bleating goats, squawking chickens, and road noise punctuated with the constant blasting of the vehicle's horn (there were no other vehicles on the road that I could see) made sporting travel. I reached for the Scotch, drawing some bad looks from the Muslims whose religion forbade alcohol. It tasted fine in the crowded heat. My brain began to relax.

Rumor, heard during an impromptu party in London's Hyde Park, suggested that there were brown trout in some streams flowing out of the mountains above Agadir. Anywhere the British went, the story went, they dragged along brown trout. I had to find out for myself, so here I was on a rickety bus bound for the mid-fourteenth century. An old man to my right laughed as I pulled on the Scotch. I'm not sure why. We turned up and into the mountains taking what I presumed was a scheduled stop somewhere thousands of feet above sea level. The bus swayed and bounced through hairpin curves at dangerous speeds. If I survived this ride, the booze wouldn't. Looking through the human chaos dancing in the aisle I could see bits and pieces of the countryside come into view and flash by through the bug-splattered windshield. Well ahead I saw a cart pulled by a donkey stopped in the middle of the road. The bus driver never hesitated and we smashed into the rig loaded with red fruit. The windshield was instantly bathed in a crimson liquid that I hoped was not blood. We rolled to a stop and people began yelling and climbing out the windows. The goats were stomping on two seats just in front of me. My man on the right opened the exit door behind the seat and bailed out. So did I. I spied the donkey struggling to its feet back down the road. The cart was shattered. There were smashed tomatoes everywhere, splattered over the road, the bus, and the donkey driver, who was now engaged in a loud discussion with the bus driver concerning some subtle nuance of road etiquette. Locals and riders alike offered considered and impassioned opinion to the debate. Hands and arms sliced the sun-blasted air making obscure points. The dialogue swiftly degenerated into physical attacks. The sound of fist hitting flesh resounded in afternoon heat. The chickens, dripping red, in the cages above launched into an inspired cacophony of avian displeasure. Life was sweet here in Morocco. This was obvious.

God, what people will do when seeking trout, I thought, as I climbed back on the bus in search of the Scotch. Eventually things were sorted out. The driver and his man smoked some more hash and three hours later we pulled into windswept, dusty Agadir-by-the-sea. The place looked like a location shot for *High Plains Drifter*. A market next to the bus station lean-to with a bench offered meat, vegetables, and bock beer at about forty cents a bottle. I bought six to go with my last jug of whiskey. I had dehydrated food but bought fruit, vegetables, and meat that might have been goat in a previous life, then filled my water bottles at a nearby fountain. My Hyde Park source had said to follow the creek by the market for three or four miles into the mountains. That is where "brown trout as big as your bloody forearm" were supposed to be. In town the creek was muddy and filled with hideous garbage. Biting flies swarmed above the turbid filth. It was late afternoon but at this time of year, early May, there was still plenty of daylight left. The road paralleling the creek soon petered out, giving way to a footpath. I proceeded up the narrow trail past small earthen homes filled with women and children who stared silently at me from the darkness within. The path veered from the creek for a couple of miles and when it returned to the water, the stream had been transformed.

Thirty feet wide and crystal clear with small cascades, pocket water, and long glides filled with green weeds that resembled watercress, the beautiful stream burbled its way into my naive heart. I could see brown trout sipping bugs near the bottom. Nymphing. The fish were from ten inches long to perhaps fifteen. Honest information about trout while on the road. In London. Amazing, and a rarity back then as well as now. Looking downstream through a vee in the hills, I could just see the dust and dull rooftops that were the tumult of Agidir. Snowless mountains rose far above me to the east in the direction of the Sahara. Scrub pine and ragged brush grew in the small park where I was standing. This was it. Exotic trout fishing. I set up a camp consisting of ground tarp, sleeping bag, and then another tarp above supported by long sticks. A small pile of wood for a fire was stacked by an old fire ring. I was not the first to fish here. I took the beer down to cool in a small eddy of the stream. It is hard to explain how good I felt, how at home, but it was one of the finest, sanest feelings in the world. Instinctively I knew this was good country, that I would be safe and happy. America was a long way away and I was alone chasing brown trout in North Africa. Youth and ignorance, a wonderful combination.

I rigged up the fly rod, an old red-glass Fenwick travel model that was rated for a six-weight line but cast like it needed a ten. Not the ideal equipment for this water, but it would do. An even older, battered Hardy Princess filled with rough fly line was secured near the butt. There were not any flies coming off the water so I opted for the Adams, a pattern that takes fish anywhere. I stepped into the stream. The water was cold, quickly soaking my Converse All-Stars and chilling my legs. There was a nice run beginning at the base of a plunge pool forty feet above me. Stripping line, the reel's noisy drag buzzed through the quiet countryside. I started fishing the nearest outside stretch of the run just a few yards upstream, hoping that superb casting and delicate presentation would allow me to take several browns from the water. Ever the dreamer.

The fly landed, floated a few feet, and was taken by a small brown, its nose just peeking through the water into the warm air. The fish leaped at the prick of the barbed hook, ran quickly, and leaped again before I grabbed it near the head. Perhaps ten inches with brown shoulders, black spots set off with a few crimson ones, and a golden belly. Twenty years or so ago catch-and-release had not reached the high dogma accorded the concept by expert and neophyte anglers of the nineties. I whacked the trout's head on my knee and tossed the fish on the bank to wait for a couple of others. Two more casts turned two more trout of the same size. I had dinner.

Across the flow was a dark eddy swirling with thin creases of mocha foam. The first Adams, one I'd tied, was tattered, its hackle unwound and mangled. I changed flies. Moving a short distance into the current for back cast room, I launched a quartering effort above the watery galaxy. The fly bobbed and bounced into the spinning pocket and a good fish took, again leaping and thrashing the surface before it sounded and drummed its head so that the vibration shot up the line to my hand with angry clarity. All four trout had been jumpers, a first for me, an individual steeped in the ignorant belief that brown trout never left the safety of the water. Since Morocco I've encountered leaping browns from the small creeks of Wisconsin to the Shields in Montana to the lava streams of Iceland. I've learned that browns will go airborne with the best of them. I pulled up on the trout and it ripped through the water, slicing downstream. I pivoted and pointed the rod in the direction of Agadir. The trout held in a small pool and I reeled my way down to the tired fish. A short run, a little head shaking, and the brown was mine—sixteen inches with the slightest suggestion of a kype on its lower jaw. It was a male, brightly colored like its smaller cousins and again with only a smattering of red spots, perhaps a half dozen along the flanks near the tail. These were beautiful, firm fish that would have done the Madison River proud. This one I released, and the act felt good and slightly noble. I still keep a few trout, usually cutthroat, for dinner when I'm camping in the high country, but killing fish has that same sense of loss and loneliness that comes with grouse hunting. I walked back to the three fish in the grass, pulled a bottle of beer from the stream, and pried the cap off with my knife. The beer foamed over the neck and down my chin as I chugged a third of the liter bottle. I can taste the taste and feel the carbonation to this day.

The trout were easy to clean—quickly cut from stern to stem, guts and gills pulled out, then quickly rinsed in the cold water.

The small pile of twigs caught fire immediately and I grilled the fish in a small pan with some sweet olive oil, garlic, salt, and pepper. The pink meat flaked from the bones tasting slightly of tannin and earth, probably from the needles of small pines growing nearby. I finished the beer, lit a Camel, leaned back on my bed roll, and thought, "I'll take fifty more years of this."

The fire went out sometime after dark and I went to sleep. At dawn the sound of crackling sticks and voices of a foreign tongue woke me. Christ! There were two Berber locals with nut-brown skin and curly black hair squatted around my fire cooking something in a fire-blackened pot. Furrowed brows focused on the bubbling concoction simmering on the coals. They were dressed in worn jeans, khaki shirts, and sandals with large sheathed knives looped to their belts. I was dead or perhaps breakfast (I've never been short on paranoia or imagination). Whatever they were cooking smelled good but more like an evening stew.

"Hello to you, sir," the heavier of the two called in good English marked by what I took to be an Arab accent. "My brother and I saw your fire last night from up there," and he pointed to a long, serrated ridge above us. "We have our goats in the new grass. Perhaps you would like some of our food?"

Waking up to this scene was a bit confusing, but I got with the program in a ragged sort of way, staggering down to the stream, retrieving a couple of bottles of the bock beer, and saying, "Sounds great. Thanks."

"Most welcome, you are," said the other and they both smiled showing bright white teeth and flashing dark eyes. "We've got bowls, but only two spoons."

The stew was hot, burning my palm through the clay bowl. I passed the beer around and ripped apart a desiccated loaf of bread to sop up the juice. I tried to remember which hand Arabs ate with, the other was used for hygienic purposes I'd been told. I gave up and ate right-handed. The knives stayed put and no one said anything. The stew was good, rich with a slight taste of wild game. My new friends were slurping up their portions.

"This is damn good. What kind of meat is it?"

"Goat. The animals are not our pets you understand," the larger one offered. "My brother and I watch our family's animals. That is our responsibility. They work in the market down below. You are the first American we've seen up here."

"How'd you know I was from the U.S. and where'd you learn to speak English?"

"You have long hair like a hippy," one replied and they both laughed. "We learned your language at school in Casa (as in blanca) but we are Berber first of all." Their pride shone in the morning light. I would not want to cross this pair over an issue of sovereignty or heritage.

I had more stew and we killed off the beer and one more bottle. They asked plenty of questions about America and I asked a few about their land. In the process I learned that the stream headed about two miles upstream forming at the outlet of a small pond fed by springs at the base of a cirquelike valley. One of them produced a stone pipe and loaded it with shavings from a dark green chunk about the size of a soap bar. Let me guess. Hash. They got the pipe smoking and took in huge lung-fulls before passing it to me. "When in Rome," as they say; coupled with the beer and the big meal, this day was off to a roaring start. They helped me break camp and insisted on carrying some of my gear as we floated up the mountain trail. An hour or so passed as in a dream before we came to the pond which was perhaps three or four acres of clear water and abundant aquatic plant growth. Trout were dimpling the surface and they weren't ten-inchers.

These were big trout. Twenty inches, maybe more, and they were sipping small mayflies. Well, hell, the Adams would fool these guys. And it did. With a cast of modest dimensions, the fly settled on the glassy surface; giving it a slight twitch, a fat brown slid over with wild nonchalance, taking my bug with an audible gulp. The tippet was plenty stout, cut back to something approximating 3X. The trout crashed and blasted around in front of us as my Berber friends, whose names I never learned, cheered lustily. This obviously beat tending goats. I dragged the fish in after a few minutes and guessed that it was twenty, twenty-one inches and over three pounds. The brown revived quickly and I let it swim free.

"What you doing? Are you crazy? You could cook that fish good for meal tonight," one of my Moroccan buddies said, genuinely upset and possibly concerned for my mental well-being.

"Maybe I'll keep one for dinner later in the day," I explained. "I just like to catch them and I could never eat more than one."

The pair stared at me dumbfounded. They were lost. One thing was clear, unmistakable—the Yankee was nuts. Out of his skull.

"Why you do this? There is no point," said the smaller one with a good deal of arm waving. Nothing about fly fishing now made sense to them and after catching and releasing several more browns, they gathered their gear and headed off to the goats. They were disappointed in me, I think, and they probably feared catching my obvious madness.

Oh well, just another day on the planet. I set up camp and caught fish until the novelty wore off sometime after dark. I did clean one brown and grilled it for dinner along with a few of the onions the Berbers had left me. A couple of cups of Scotch cooled with pond water made for a pleasant night under a sky packed with stars and a few shooters that sizzled over the peaks above.

"That's the size of it Talia," I said, filling the glasses one more time. "I spent a couple of weeks there and I found two other streams, just as good as the first. No one had fished them in years. I bet no one has since either. What do you think?"

"I think you're nuts, but if you can put the trip together, I'll go," said Talia.

"No problem. Next year for sure. The night wound on and we turned our attention to John's Missouri Breaks elk hunt once again. Tomorrow we'd fish the midge hatch.

The next day was overcast but temperatures were headed into the forties, ideal midge weather. Bermuda shorts and martinis on the veranda at dusk. By midafternoon the sun was playing games with the Bitterroot, slipping from behind the cloud cover to blast its warming rays on the river. There were open spots in the ice—irregularly shaped circles where eddies spun in the summer and rectangular slots that exposed deep runs. We would work these with pupae imitations first and maybe dries later.

Dressed in polypropylene long underwear, jeans, wool shirts, sweaters, hats, fingerless mittens, and bulky neoprene waders, we cut a dashing sight as we trundled down to the river, clumping through a foot or so of snow. I felt like the Michelin tire man. The water, what there was of it that was even marginally fishable, covered perhaps a couple of hundred yards of stream course. Talia went upstream and I punched through rotten ice into the gravel shallows directly in front of me. The pupa imitation was weighted. I derricked it into the head of the slot, hoping to sink and dredge the minuscule bug in front of a shocked rainbow or brown. The first few casts were fun in a frigid novel way, especially when the sun came out for a minute or two. Then the air warmed quickly with cruel hints of spring that was still several weeks down the road. After awhile the fishing became routine—cast upstream, mend slightly, follow the drift, dig out the line, and cast again. I worked the entire width and length of the run thoroughly, then began to repeat the process. One more time and then back to the lodge for a warm beverage.

After about the twentieth drift, the line stopped, an action that went unnoticed until I started to lift the line for another cast. First feeling like cobbled streambed, the resistance suddenly took on life and began to figure-eight and zig-zag about the run. I feared for the leader when the fish dragged it beneath the ice's sharp edge. Soon the trout tired. In the cold and dark, the fish's metabolism was probably running at about 10 percent. Still, it was a trout on a fly in winter, a brief touch with the year's angling to come. I crunched my way to the run and lifted the rod as high as possible, pulling the trout to me. Dark, silvery with a puckered mouth. Damn. A mountain whitefish. I should have known. The species loves patterns like these worked deep. What the hell.

Fourteen inches (a certain sickness attends anyone measuring a whitefish) and a native to the waters. I let the fish go and it sunk from sight. I'd had enough. So had Talia. He'd been lucky, though. He caught nothing.

The evening was more of the night before and we made plans to meet on the Blackfeet Reservation in May for some big-trout fishing. Talia had to return to the West Coast and work. I was going home to catch up on some writing before driving down to Arizona and the Grand Canyon. It had been twenty years since I last hiked there—far too long.

Running along Highway 64 through the Kaibab Forest brought back memories of a similar excursion a couple of decades back. Little had changed in this part of Arizona, unlike that populous devastation meted out to the Tucson and Phoenix areas. I would not be going to those places again in this lifetime. The drive down from Montana had taken me through a variety of late winter storms and pleasant flashes of springtime. Here fresh snow dripped from the needles and limbs of the small pines covering the flats and rough hills. The sun was out and the air had warmed into the fifties on this early March morning. The scents of pine and sage were in the crisp air. I had planned to be in the region sooner, but some late assignments held things up. It is amazing how much food three children can walk out of a refrigerator in one week. Life after forty is different than life at twenty. Denying myself that first mind-blowing look into the canyon for the moment, I raced through Canyon Village, a collection of Park Service buildings, tourist attractions, and other operations dedicated to the proposition that travelers and money needn't spend much time together and, axiomatically, if this is a National Park, the human race is duty bound to erect as much tacky, tasteless crap as possible within its borders. I can safely report that we were doing a fine job on that front at Grand Canyon.

A friend of mine who guides rafters on the river told me over some wine one evening that hikers now needed permits to wander the canyon's backcountry. The same holds true for Glacier Park just east of my home. I do not believe in permits when it comes to wilderness.

"Will that be one night or two?" asks an officiously saccharine voice hiding beneath an institutionally gray uniform.

"What?"

"Smoking or nonsmoking, sir?"

"What?"

"You've been assigned lot number 9 at Hole-in-the-Wall Campground, sir. Right next to the brown metal bear-proof food storage locker and within sight of the outhouse. You're quite lucky today."

"I can see that."

"Oh! and sir ..."

"Yes."

"Remember, no campfires, fishing, drinking, or smoking, sir."

"What time is PT?"

"O-six-hundred, sir."

"Christ!"

That is how things go these days as the thundering horde descends on some of the better country in the West, but I ignore the permit process. I was headed for Fish Creek Trail about seventeen miles from the quaint village. The road wound through grassy sage flats. It was salmon, ochre dirt made muddy from the snow on top but bone dry just below. Antelope jackrabbits with huge ears bounded and soared in front and alongside the truck as we bounced along at 25 mph. The juniper and pinyon pines were short, maybe twenty feet tall at most. The day was warming and the land was drying out. Memories came back of my first trip here so long ago. I'd been away too long. Pulling over just below a fire lookout not so far from the Fish Creek Trail, I scrounged around for a Pabst in the cooler and climbed the flights of stairs to the top. Being a world-class acrophobe, the height bothered me at first. Then I crept to the edge of the railing and looked out.

No one can adequately describe the Grand Canyon. It is immense beyond comprehension, and ancient. The colors are staggering. Red, pink, gold, orange, gray, blue —the colors all winking in subtle and fantastic shadings as clouds and sunlight conspire in natural madness. Spectacular doesn't quite explain the canyon. *Time and the River Flowing* by Francois Leydet or Colin Fletcher's *The Man Who Walked Through Time* hint at the power here and are worth reading. But they are only brief glimpses, snapshots of what is really out there.

I'd planned on spending a week or so at the bottom of the canyon. The last time I'd spent two weeks and when I finally struggled out (the walk up is a bitch), I had difficulty speaking to people. I'd spent too much time alone. Ordering a porterhouse steak rare, onion rings, and a beer in the village was tough. Everyone else was running at a faster clip than I was. Thinking in civilized terms seemed foreign. Down along the Colorado River I'd lived on rice, beans, dried apricots, granola (a sad statement, I admit), and grilled carp fillets, the fish taken on both nymphs and doughballs manufactured from the trail mix. The rainbow fishing below Lee's Ferry is superb, but I wanted to go back in time and catch carp again. There were lots of trout back in Montana. I drank the river water without ill effect back then. This time around I carried the same provisions but without the tent or a camera, cutting the weight so that I could bring a few cans of beer and a bottle of Jack Daniels—hedonistic priorities asserting themselves at over four thousand feet above the canyon floor.

I drank in the view, finished off the beer, and headed down the canyon. The pack was already loaded except for the beer. The rest of my gear was locked in the cab. I parked the rig out of sight behind a copse of pines, shouldered the backpack, heavy as hell but I was going downhill (as I'd been told many times recently), and started down to the river nearly ten miles away.

Unlike Bright Angel Trail, which resembles an inner city thoroughfare peopled with garishly attired touristas either walking or riding burros who have managed to leave sufficient road apples to alleviate any problems with dust (a damn nice aroma on a warm day, too), the Fish Creek Trail is rarely traveled. The path starts out obviously enough, working its way down to a sandy plateau before losing itself among exposed rock. Then it plunges precariously down along red rock cliffs. The view

of the inner canyon is stunning. I stopped and took in the sight as afternoon clouds dropped thin sheets of rain on pinnacles of rock. Here was where I'd seen a cougar playing with a piece of tumbleweed in the late afternoon light many years back. The animal ranged back and forth batting the dead plant much like a house cat with a ball of yarn. I can still picture the sprays of red dust the cat kicked up as it romped about oblivious to my presence. Below the rock walls, the trail winds through cactus, brush, and yucca for several miles. A smooth, water-worn streambed was a reminder of the dangers of sudden squalls and flash floods. The fauna of the canyon down here is Lower Sonoran and consists of creatures adapted to desert conditions. I spotted little earless lizards, chuckwalla, leopard lizards, a couple of tiny deer, a bright orange female collared lizard, and a black-and-white Boyle's king snake. Serrated indentations in the dust trailing behind serpentine markings indicated the passage of a Grand Canyon rattlesnake. There were also antelope, ground squirrels, eagles, ravens, songbirds, desert wood rats, pocket mice (campsite pests), kangaroo rats, ring-tailed cats, spotted skunks, and bighorn sheep. Obviously this was good, healthy country.

Finally, after several hours of dusty walking, water gone, I heard the river rushing through the gorge. Soon I spotted the Colorado a thousand feet below. I followed remnants of the Tonto Trail that parallels the river until I came to a field of rock and boulder that opened to the water. On the first trip a friend of mine had almost dropped over a dry fall in the dark in a crazed, dehydrated search for water. He realized just in time that the water was many feet below and we slept on the trail until dawn. Water never tasted so good as it did that morning. This time the scramble down to the river took twenty minutes. The beach where I planned to camp was smaller than I remembered. Perhaps shrunk by upstream dam operations or exaggerated by my hyperbolic memory. I set up camp well above the river in much the same way as I did in Morocco. The method had worked for years now. I'd allowed three beers per day. A lot of weight coming in and my legs were tired, but the beer would be gone before I climbed back out making for a friendlier pack. I opened one and worked at it while I rigged up a six-weight graphite traveler rod, a far cry from the red-glass Fenwick. I tied on a large, Gold-Ribbed Hare's Ear and slid across the bone-colored sand to the river that was running low and clear in the evening warmth. Even in March the temperature can reach eighty between the walls that radiate heat like a solar oven.

I was using a sink-tip line and some weight. The first cast went well upriver and the fly walked itself along the smooth bottom of a soft eddy along the bank. I let the fly work around, giving the rod slight taps and lifts every so often. Soon I was rewarded with a couple of tugs and a take. The line cut through the water out into the current. I pulled back and more line whizzed off the reel. The fish went way downstream and I followed across the beach and then the jumble of rocks. A smaller sandbar poked into the river and it was here that I saw the fish. Large. Ten pounds at least, with grayish-silver on the flanks and a yellow belly. The fins were tipped in subdued red that indicated spawning was underway. The carp of my dreams. I was elated that the species was still here. The fish made a couple more strong runs that I managed to check with 2X-tippet bravery. Carp are stronger though less acrobatic fish than trout. A ten-pound carp would smoke a similar-sized rainbow in a tug of war. The water was cool as I stepped in and tailed the exhausted fish. Well over ten pounds. Maybe thirteen or fourteen. I had dinner and quickly sliced large fillets of more than a pound each from the flanks. I threw the remains up into the rocks and brush for the rodents, ants, and other bugs. Carp have always held a special place in my angling life dating back to the days when friends and I used to catch them on whiskey doughballs in the Rock River of northern Illinois. I've taken large ones in Lake Michigan near Bailey's Harbor in Wisconsin and in some European waters, where the fish is considered sophisticated sport.

Carp In North America by the American Fisheries Society is still one of my favorite books.

Dusk was giving way to night by the time the small fire of bleached sticks had burned down to orange coals. I draped the fillets over a small grill, coating them with a touch of olive oil seasoned with some salt, pepper, and sage. They cooked quickly, leaving barely enough time to retrieve a can of mandarin orange slices from the river. I ate these from the can and picked chunks of the fish off the grill that I'd taken off the fire. A couple of quarts of the Colorado had been pumped through a small purifier and some of this liquid washed down the meal. As good as any I'd ever had. Nothing like several pounds of grilled carp to replenish depleted energy reserves. Food cooked in the wild and eaten alone takes on heightened flavor and importance.

A handful of twigs caught flame swiftly, illuminating the sand and rock walls behind me. I poured a splash of Jack in a cup and sat back to enjoy the stars winking in the crease of sky above me. The fire's gold light shone on the rock walls and danced on the river. There was only the sound of the moving water and the poppings from the fire. I was alone. No one to talk to. No one to help if I broke a leg. A perfect setting. The stroll in had taken a toll and I drifted off as the sky appeared to drop into the canyon. The soft glow of dawn found me in the same position as when I'd nodded off. The sleep of the dead is a rare and appreciated gift.

Breakfast was the remaining carp now chilled from the night and a quart of Tang plus a few vitamins. The juice tastes awful but is easy to pack and has some vitamin C. Don't want to catch scurvy in the wilderness.

On the earlier trip I'd located the remains of the old Fish mining operation. Some rusting tools, pieces of rotted saddle leather and harness, and a few cooking utensils. Chances of this spot producing a mother lode of gold appeared slim and I never found much in the way of tailings. Fish was probably a hermit of more disciplined habit than myself, the mining an excuse to escape society. I climbed the gray cliff where I'd last seen the mining paraphernalia and reached it after a mild workout. I turned and watched the river run below me. The water had risen in the night and was just a touch milky. The rusting metal was still here but the leather tack was gone, perhaps eaten or completely disintegrated. Finding these artifacts was a direct touch with the past and exciting. I felt vaguely connected to Fish and wondered what he looked like. Old? Young? Probably skinny? Bearded? On the run from the law? Who knew? I'd try to find a picture in a book in the Whitefish library, even though locating one was a long shot.

After a couple of hours I returned to camp, grabbed the rod, and walked a quarter-mile upstream. The sound of helicopters reached me in a dim "whomp-whomp-whomp." I hated them anywhere and more so when they intruded on my solitude. Tourists too damn lazy to walk hired these helicopters to see the canyon in decadent style. A twin-engine airplane also crossed my strip of sky. More tourists. Reading about these planes crashing always upset me deeply. Right. Nothing took my nymph for an hour or so and the day was clear and hot. Time for a nap, then a bit of angling near sunset.

Hours later. First cast. In the same eddy. Another long- running, downstream fight and another large carp.

Dinner almost served. A person could get spoiled on this life in a week, I hoped. Some chili accompanied the fish tonight along with a bottle of Soave. How did that get in the pack? More fire and starry sky and more deadhead sleep. By day three I was completely rested and relaxed.

The week was spent much like the first couple of days with brief trips of five or six miles up and down the river along the Tonto Trail. The unfathomable age of the surroundings, billions of years of history lay in the rock, blasted away my ego. Awareness of the daily routine was heightened but almost all sense of personality disappeared. No longer was John Holt the person calling an editor in New York to hustle an assignment, nor was John Holt the person swearing at a crazed Montana driver. John Holt the person was gone. A welcome relief that served as benefit to no one in particular. Eating, fishing, hiking, staring into space were just activities to be enjoyed instant by instant. By day eight a sense of loneliness became noticeable, a sure indication that the time was right to climb out of the canyon. Most of the food was gone as was the beer and the Jack. I'd found what I'd come looking for and had discovered that perhaps you can go home again if your expectations are realistic. This visit brought clear and vivid memories of my earlier trek, but this time the experience was slightly different, perhaps better and more enjoyable. It was hard to say.

The pack was much lighter and the hike out seemed easier. I even spied the rare blooming of a century plant growing on a little sandy flat above the creek bed. I was beat by the time I reached the first plateau just below where the truck was parked. Hot. Sweaty. The last mile of switchbacks was hell and I was reduced to moaning and brief trudges of fifty yards or less. The winter workouts on the exercise bike had helped but not enough. I staggered out of the canyon and weaved to the truck. The pack crashed into the bed. After a week the water left in the cooler smelled strange. Warm beer wasn't much better but it quenched my thirst. A windmill near a small abandoned ranch or ranger station was pumping parsimonious amounts of water into a stock tank. I shed my clothes and climbed in. The cold nearly stopped my heart and bore into my brain. The last of the sun dried my skin and I changed into fresh clothes for the obligatory foray into the moron madness that is Canyon Village.

Marauding herds of jackrabbits sprang through the beams of the headlights. Deer, eyes glowing, looked out from the trees. All too soon the glare of arc and neon lights from the "real" world lit up the road now turned from dirt to pavement. I parked in back of the main lodge and walked into the rustic restaurant, which actually still retained a passable, even pleasant, atmosphere.

The waitress came up silently and stared for a moment.

"You've been in the canyon alone, haven't you," she stated with dead clear eyes. I was finished. "I can always tell. I spend every spare moment down there myself. Why else would I put up with this place." Her bemused look said it all, and I still hadn't said anything. "I'll bring you a beer," she said and did.

"Give me the porterhouse rare with onion rings, please," I said, quite happy with my eloquence. She placed the order and returned with another icy mug. I sipped it and watched the visitors from the safety of my nook in a dark corner. Man, why do all these guys look like escapees from a National Lampoon movie? Garish shorts. Hideous T-shirts with catchy phrases like Ski Iraq. Pointed hats with long pink feathers. Cheap sandals. My right hand instinctively started searching for the 9mm pistol that was nowhere to be found.

"Here you are," my friend said, placing a plate of sizzling, juicy meat and crisp onion rings in front of me. Another beer appeared. I was in love. The steak was a delicious change from the carp. Finished, I paid the bill, left a five-hundred-dollar tip and staggered out to the truck. I drove to a parking lot overlook away from the village and pitched my sleeping bag near the rim out of sight of passing motorists and amorous village employees. In two days I'd be home in Montana. The fishing would be on the rise and I missed Lynda and the kids. I'd call them in the morning. The Colorado was a barely audible roar far below in the darkened canyon which radiated the slightest turquoise glow. Coming back next year seemed like a good idea, but waiting for ten years or so seemed even better.

Some places are so fine a person needs time to comprehend what he has experienced.

Mid-March is a time of great expectation. Spring is only days away and there is the real possibility of decent weather ahead. Large, dirty piles of snow along the sides of roads and around the edges of my driveway are grim reminders of snowplows, whiteouts, and the dark, cold season. March skies are more often cloudy than blue in Montana as weather patterns begin to shift from frigid arctic blasts to more temperate systems drifting in from the Pacific. For the past several years March and April have also meant Skwalas, an obscure stonefly that triggers voracious feeding activity in big trout on rivers throughout the western third of the state.

The Skwala is known mainly among die-hard fly fishers in Montana. Little has been written about the bug even in the scientific community. The one-inch-and-some-change long insect is a member of the family Perlodidae and the genus *Isoperla*, and that is about the extent of the written information on the species in books in my library other than a mention in passing by Gary LaFontaine in *The Art of the Dry Fly*. I first learned of the hatch some years ago from a friend when we fished the Bitterroot River during the early part of March. Putting in around one o'clock we spent the first hour casting for fun and few if any trout as the raft slid along in the current. Around two o'clock, helped considerably by the sun, big browns and rainbows along with a few carefree cutthroat began slurping the emerging bugs near gravel and rock shorelines. Some of the biggest trout of the year, fish of twenty-seven inches, are taken on Skwala imitations. I've taken a few trout over twenty inches and a number in the eighteen-to-nineteen-inch range. All eager, feisty fish. The rainbows are often in prespawning color—flaming red, gunmental silver, jet black spots, soft iridescent purple. Wonderful fish.

I've never seen the stoneflies airborne. Perhaps they are flightless. They definitely prefer emerging on

the rocky cobble. The sun-warmed, relatively flat surfaces probably facilitate the drying of their bodies.
Bankside structure such as this will always hold the
insects and the fishing is dependable year after year as
long as the river does not change the nature of the
streambed. The majority of fly fishing during this hatch
takes place on the Bitterroot but the upper Clark Fork,
Rock Creek, Blackfoot, and Middle Fork of the Flathead
rivers have also produced trout for me on Skwalas.

My friend has his own pattern that uses a gray
foam body. I now tie an Elk Hair Caddis on a long-
shanked dry fly hook using gray hair, gray dubbing and
thread, and a palmered Cree hackle. It looks like a drab
salmonfly but catches fish even in summer.

I try to fish the hatch on the Bitterroot each year
in part because I love the river and the country and also
because I have friends down that way. Skwalas are some-

thing of a springtime rendezvous. Now that I've discovered the bugs on the Middle Fork and some smaller tributaries of the upper Clark Fork, I direct more attention to those waters since they are closer to home and more accessible.

The Middle Fork begins in the Great Bear Wilderness south of Glacier Park. The river is wild for much of its length, with pure, slightly sterile water from a nutrient standpoint. After running out of the Great Bear, the Middle Fork is more or less paralleled by U.S. 2. A bit of hiking and the river returns to its pristine character most of the time. There is a fine run of nearly a mile less than twenty miles from home. Large rainbows, native westslope cutthroat, and hybrids of the two are found in good numbers. The water is rarely fished. The locals prefer to hit the lakes and rivers, like Flathead and the Kootenai, which have better reputations. Pine forest and rock outcroppings dominate the northern bank. Colorful rocks worn smooth from tumbling in the current are piled up in unstable banks and bars on the southern side. This is where I fish. The peaks of Glacier are visible to the east. Black and grizzly bears are not uncommon here. Eagles ride the thermals far above. Deer and elk graze on the lush grasses of the meadows and wetlands. Ravens mark time eerily in the trees.

Arriving at the river after noon, I saw a number of trout feeding along a deep, swift run opposite me. The sun was out more often than not as dark, thick clouds rushed toward the high plains forty miles east over the mountains.

Working out fifty feet of line, the first cast landed well above the run but a little short of the feeding lane. I decided to fish it out anyway. The water was aquamarine but crystal clear so I could easily observe the silvery form of a large fish rising up from the bottom. The rise took forever and the trout grew in size with each passing instant. The fish's mouth was open and the gray Elk Hair disappeared as the rainbow engulfed it standing on its tail in the water column. I eagerly, overzealously per- haps, set the hook. The trout catapulted into the air and smacked the surface with a big-fish "whack." A powerful

sound. Normally rainbows like this one leap a bit then sound, running downstream. This fish opted for an up- stream, near-surface, high-intensity flight for freedom. Line zipped from the reel. I should have followed but figured, incorrectly, that the trout's run would be short- lived because of the current. Not so. The fish went well into the backing and thrashed in some gravelly shallows seventy-five yards above me. The river bent to my right and line rubbed across dry rock. Reeling, slipping and sliding as I moved upstream, tension was restored to the line. Luck and the good life. The rainbow leaped three times in quick succession when I tried to horse it down to the calm water at my feet.

The fish held on the edge of the main flow and I regained the backing and most of the fly line before the creature saw me and charged downstream. As it rocketed by I could see that this was a legitimate twenty-inch trout—my first of the year and I did not want to lose it. Of course it would be set free, but not being able to hold the rainbow in my hands, to feel it try and shake loose from my grasp, would be a disappointment. So I scrambled back down river coming perilously close to falling in the icy water as the rocks gave way like quicksand beneath my feet. I checked the fish before it reached the others that were still feeding aggressively. I wanted to catch a few more of these guys—angler's greed shining in the late-winter light.

Pulling back slightly with the five-weight, the trout rose up and leaped one more time. A total of five jumps. Slowly the line came in. The leader was at the rod tip. With rod arched and held high, I stooped over and secured the rainbow by the tail. A male in full, blood-red spawning display, probably on the move to mate in one of the small feeder creeks nearby. Its back was slightly humped. The makings of a serious kype were underway with the lower jaw already hooking upwards. I laid the fish against the rod and noted its length so I could later measure it with a tape. Knowing the size of a fish is part of the fun and helps in recollecting events to friends over drinks. Reviving the trout took a couple of minutes of patient, careful ministration before the tail muscles flexed in my grip and the rainbow was gone. Just like that. I'd had ten or fifteen minutes of contact, a long time in trout fishing, and then there was nothing except the memory of the leaps and those intense colors. That was always more than enough.

Sitting on the bank with my feet in the water, I pulled the tape from a coat pocket and stretched it along the rod. Twenty-three inches. A very good trout, maybe five pounds. Other decent rainbows were working twenty feet from me. I saw several Skwalas crawling on the rocks nearby. Farther away, close to the far shore, cutthroat were feeding on what looked like dark caddis. The wild and unsophisticated cutts were slurping, splashing, and creating a general racket over there in contrast to the more disciplined but no less intense efforts of the rainbows. The air had warmed to the sixties and I shed my jacket. The sun beat down on the land and the sound of melting, running water was everywhere. Spring was here for now. Sounds of breaking twigs and clattering rocks reached me from the trees across the Middle Fork. Pebbles and dirt slid into the water. Elk I hoped but wondered if a grizzly was foraging in the south-facing slope, its mind still goofy from the extended winter dormancy. The animal continued upstream. I could follow its course by the noise of its passage somewhere out of sight in the woods. Sometime later while releasing another rainbow, the fishing was good and easy this day, I spotted a ratty-looking black bear loping across a decrepit wooden bridge several hundred yards upstream. Where the animal was headed was anyone's guess—perhaps into town for a burger and fries or whatever else was in the dumpster behind the restaurant.

By now I'd either exercised or put down all of the rainbows in the stretch. No more Skwalas were visible but the cutthroat were still working away on the far bank. I changed to a #14 brown Elk Hair after dropping the tippet from 4X to 5X. Using the dependable Elk Hair ensured some measure of success. The cast was seventy-five feet and required a reach to compensate for current and gain a few feet of float in the process. One-hundred-foot casts are for the experts and anything over eighty feet or so was pushing my limits with a five- or six-weight rod. The initial offering was short and fishless. The next was closer to the mark but did not cover the trout that fed only on the insects emerging directly in their line of sight. When nature is throwing food in your face, why struggle? The third cast was on the money and a cutthroat nailed the fly, running swiftly for the sanctity of the bottom, then coming with a head-shaking struggle, across the river to my eager hand. Largely cold-silver in color with hundreds of black spots, the fish was fat even by summer standards and seventeen inches long. A few caddis spilled out of its mouth when I lifted the fish from the water—a salmonid glutton—and fine trout. Working down the run, three more of the same general dimensions pounced on the fly.

A few hours fishing under ideal conditions pro-duced a dozen trout from fifteen to twenty-three inches. I could live with that, especially with the hard-earned knowledge that days like this were far from my angling norm.

If fly fishing was always stone cold easy, what would be the intrigue, the fun? Snipping off the fly, I turned and started back up the river toward the truck.

SPRING

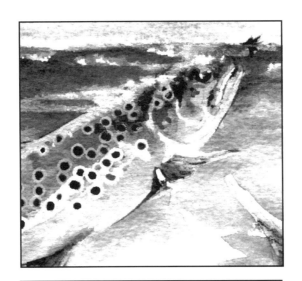

THE GAME
HEATS UP

THE GAME
HEATS UP

S pring is a sometime situation in Montana. There will be a run of sunny days in the sixties filled with reports of temperatures in the upper eighties at places like Glasgow and Baker and Miles City in the eastern section of the state. Similar weather shows up west of the Rocky Mountains, though temperature shifts are not as dramatic, averaging in the lower sixties and sometimes reaching into the seventies. The first flush days of warmth are chaotic, joyous affairs marked by shirt sleeves, cold drinks on the back deck in the sunshine, and eager plans for future fishing expeditions.

Talia had just called firming up the dates for the Blackfeet Reservation later on and we also worked out a schedule for turkey hunting and fishing in Bighorn country, in the Paradise Valley, and along the Madison and Ruby rivers. This voyage had the makings of an epic filled with a couple of thousand miles of road time, many long days fishing, and plenty of good food and drink in prime country. I could hardly wait, but five weeks is only five weeks. Talia was a tax consultant, a shortcoming most of us were able to overlook, and was entering crunch time culminating in the madness of the April 15 filing deadline. I had caught up on my writing and had several proposals pending, so I was free to fish and read and sit idly and fish some more. Lynda loved these periods dearly when my attentions centered on tying northern pike flies and wondering when the clouds would return bringing with them some aggressive pike on the early-season spawn.

Northerns were illegally introduced in Montana years ago and have had negative effects on trout populations, but not to the degree that, say, muskies have on walleyes (basically an overgrown perch with the fighting characteristics of bread dough) in Wisconsin. The primitive predators grow to over thirty pounds in places like the Flathead and Whitefish rivers only minutes from home. I caught literally thousands of these fish as a kid, mostly in Ontario. As a result, the current fly fishing mania for northern has passed me by for the most part. Pike fever is so strong in the state that packs of normally sedate trout guides from places like Dillon drive en masse up this way in the spring to fling twelve-inch streamers into likely looking holes. This year I'd decided to make a token effort at the latest in fly fishing hipness.

Last year friends of mine went chasing pike on the Northern Cheyenne Indian Reservation well east of the Little Bighorn Battlefield and a long way from any Holiday Inn that I know. They found a creek that was stuffed with northerns and the landowners generously gave them permission to fish the turbid little stream. (I've since waded the stream and it is several miles of brown, mucky, brush-choked stagnation with a few springs tossed in for variety, but it sure does have pike in it.) According to my friend's report, on one cast along an overgrown bank, a northern came screaming upstream like a Trident submarine and attacked the streamer. An ugly fight ensued that led to a shattered eight-weight, shredded waders, chewed up ankles, and, as my friend tells it, "When the damn fish bit me he had to die, so I stuck him with my knife." The pictures of the event are not pretty. My friend is not Don Johnson and the pike didn't look all that good either—toothy mouth agape (the northern), blood running down its flanks and along my friend's arms. But then nothing ever comes easy for my friend.

A low pressure system did sweep into the Flathead Valley by Tuesday, bringing with it low-flying clouds that hid the mountains in dark gray, purplish scum. Light drizzle ruled the day. Perfect pike weather and I knew an excellent spot a couple of miles from the front door. The streamer was a bunch of spun white deer hair and long clumps of red and white marabou. The body was silver ribbed tinsel. The whole thing was weighted with fuse wire. I'd patterned my life after Theodore Gordon years ago. Working the line out was an ungainly process and the casts landed in the river with the delicacy of a road-killed skunk dropped from the second-floor balcony of a Best Western Inn. This was fine. The commotion would attract not frighten the northerns that were by and large a surly lot dedicated to eating anything that moved.

The water was a murky cream jade and the flashing of the streamer on retrieve was just visible. In Canada a method that often worked was making long, fast strips followed by quick darting ones and then pausing to let the whole mess drop through the water. The same method worked here. Pike are so fast it is unsettling. One minute there is nothing. Then "wham!" they come out of nowhere and tear the fly with elongated jaws studded with thousands of mean-looking, razor-sharp teeth. (Years ago I saw the mangled hand of a man who had tried to unhook a plug from a pike that was still alive and angry. It was a gory sight.) The rod jerked down, almost out of my hands, and I yanked just as hard in the opposite direction.

The pike rushed to the surface and wagged its head above the water, gills flaring red, water spraying silvery across the river's surface. How could I have forgotten the rush of hooking up with this species? The northern pulled a good deal of line from the reel, then dogged it down deep out of sight. The fish stopped short of a tangle of limbs lodged in an earthen cutbank elbow of the river. Then it ran toward me and I tried to keep pace with the slack. I almost made it before the fish raced across stream, crashing into the bank and turning that

portion of the river muddy. Water slopped up onto the bank. Dropping the rod down to the right and jerking back, I threw the fish off balance and I quickly repeated the process on the left. The pike was stunned. I reeled it quickly to me, smacking the fish on the head with a water-soaked limb I found in the river. The soggy wood splintered but the northern was coldcocked, out like a light. I was using twenty-five pound tippet (more of Gordon's influence here) allowing me to hoist the pike partially out of the water. Dropping the rod, I kicked and shoved the fish up the bank into the green grass, not a sight common to the Beaverkill. The northern was over twelve pounds—long, thick, olive drab with dirty cream marks running lengthwise along its flanks. The fins along the back of the body were tinged with bronze. The pectorals were gold and the belly was yellow fading to off-white. Northerns are excellent when filleted, grilled over hot coals, and served with lemon wedges and roughly ground black pepper. That was the fate waiting for this one.

A late start on the fishing meant that dark was closing in, prime time for big pike, but I was unfamiliar with this stretch of river and, until I learned more, I'd pass on the nighttime hunting. There would be other days and this had been a nice outing to reacquaint myself with the northern pike.

Taking fish on the first cast is a peculiarity common to spring. Trout have spent a winter of dormancy beneath the ice, lurking in the cold darkness of winter. They are hungry, on the prowl, and unwary. Several months of pounding from anglers casting an array of patterns, plugs, baits, and other objects are required before the trout relearn the ancient art of selectivity and caution. A couple of small lakes near Whitefish come to mind when I think of first-cast success.

One of them is a catch-and-release-only lake approximately twenty-five minutes away. The water is cold, deep, fertile, and holds fair numbers of rainbows that run anywhere from ten inches to more than two feet. The lake is quite popular with local fly fishers including myself. A good day here would be five fish averaging eighteen inches in two hours fishing. The only drawback to it is that the Department of Fish, Wildlife and Parks occasionally dumps huge, old, exhausted brood stock in the water. This in itself is fine. The fish quickly rejuvenate, regaining muscle tone and a bright, silvery color. They become quality game fish within months. Unfortunately the department also makes sure news of the plantings is blasted over the airwaves and printed in every valley newspaper. This draws hordes of bait fishers who lob worms, salmon eggs, corn, and leeches into the lake. Trout caught never see the water again. The enforcement of the catch-and-release regulation here is a joke, and has seriously hurt a fishery that could be outrageously good. Despite this, good fishing can still be had by those who spend time learning the water.

Where I park my truck is at the end of an old logging road beneath some large pines that overlook the lake and a small grassy knoll. This location is also the scene of many teenage beer parties and I spend a number of hours each year picking up cans, bottles, cigarette butts, and items associated with safe sex. Life blossoms in many forms in the Rockies.

The most productive way to fish the water is from a float tube and I have acquired several over the years. My current favorite is called a U-Boat and is designed for easy entrance and egress, no mean consideration when wearing swim fins and chest waders. The U-Boat has an open end, unlike the conventional donut-shaped affair that is nearly impossible to make a quick exit from the water for purposes of bladder relief. The sight of an angler frantically clambering out of his tube, then clomping and tripping like a hunched-over duck as he heads desperately into the trees, is comical when observed from a distance. The first minutes of floating are used to shake out gear and get used to fishing from 1 $\frac{1}{2}$ feet above water level. Casting is more difficult this close to the surface, but the compensation is that trout are far less suspicious of someone trying to catch them while suspended in their element than they are of those winging stuff at them from a canoe or standing on shore. To my way of thinking, float tubes are a marvelous invention.

The first day one is legally allowed to fish this lake is April 1. Snowmobilers have been hammering the trout for months through the ice unencumbered by legal constraints or ethical considerations. I spot a number of dead rainbows lying in the weeds cloaking the lake's bottom as I paddle to a small hole in last year's dead aquatic plant growth. I can still see ice and snow along the shore sheltered from the sun. The air temperature is maybe forty-five degrees, with the water around forty. Trout are more active at closer to fifty, but the fish should be on the feed by now. A five-weight rod with a ten-foot sink-tip line and a leader tapered to 5X works well with this type of fishing. The longer tip gives the Biggs Special (a dynamite damselfly nymph imitation) a more natural appearance as it is moved up and down the water column. The Biggs is one fly I will never be without when fishing lakes, ponds, and reservoirs. When damsels and dragonflies are present in a water, the pattern is guaranteed to take fish. The tie also imitates various caddis pupae and mayfly nymphs. Just a twist or two of brown hackle at the bend of a #10 3X hook, a body of size 0 olive chenille, and a few barbules of mallard flank feather tied in on top. The fly looks like nothing when dry but takes on a tantalizing life of its own in the water.

The clear spot I was going to cast to held a small spring that cooled the water in the summer and warmed it in the cold of early April. I worked out some line and launched the Biggs toward the shore side of the pool.

Just as the line and fly touched the surface the water erupted in a large explosion. Startled, I involuntarily jerked the rod back, but the rainbow was already hooked, running for dear life and a bed of reeds to my left. I clamped the drag down tightly and the fish pulled up short of the obstruction. I heaved and could not budge the trout even with four-pound strength in the tippet. The fish was holding steady in the water. The line thrummed under the strain. The standoff lasted a couple of minutes before the fish let go of the water and sliced through the still surface into the air.

"Holy shit," I muttered.

Easily the biggest rainbow I'd connected with at this lake. The trout ran again and then, as is depressingly common to big, lake-born trout, it swam meekly to the net which was too small to land the fish. I tailed the fat, wide-shouldered rainbow. Both the fish and I were in stunned suspension of belief. The trout due to his unfortunate predicament. I because the trout stretched several inches over each end of the eighteen-inch mark on the float tube apron. Putting the fish in the water, I submerged the rod and marked the trout from the end of the grip to well up toward the first guide of its nine-foot length. The rainbow, a big hen obviously pardoned from the state hatchery, had regained a good deal of her noble status as a wild trout. She tugged at my grip and powered away from sight at her release. Pulling the plastic tape from a pocket of the tube I measured twenty-six inches and a touch more. Four inches longer than my previous longest here and easily over five pounds; perhaps seven. I began to think that this would be my year for big trout.

Three hours later the excitement of that fish had faded. I was cold and one foot was wet from a tiny cut in the waders. I prudently paddled to shore and dragged the gear to the truck. There was a Thermos of hot, very strong Ethiopian coffee in the cab. I'd become a coffee snob according to Lynda, but this brew is so good it should be illegal. Acid-free caffeine without the shakes that can turn you on like a switch. I was addicted. Dry socks and jeans plus the coffee warmed the body. A strong Honduran cigar stimulated the senses. Why complain. The day featured a damn big rainbow by anybody's standards and an entire season of fishing lay ahead.

But the angling gods are a fickle, capricious bunch and that was to be the only fish I caught in several outings at this little wooded gem until late summer. You take the fish where you find them, I guess.

Several of my fly fishing companions have tired of my touting the Biggs Special, also known as a Sheep Creek, but one doubter was converted at a small pond west of Kalispell (a town slightly larger than Whitefish a dozen miles south) in early April. The ranch pond is open to the public due to the generosity of its owner and the fact that the water is state stocked with strong, solid rainbows. This one Sunday was cool but sunny and a couple of families were eagerly plying their bait fishing trade on the near shore as we closed the gate by the gravel road and dragged our float tubes, fins, and rods to the shore. The first hour was fruitless as we cast and trolled a variety of mayfly nymphs and caddis pupae imitations. There were no bugs on the water.

When in doubt in places like this I tie on the Biggs, a one-trick pony at its finest. If damsels were present, and I was sure that they were, the fish would feed on the nymphs throughout the year as they crawled along the pond's bottom. I began casting the fly tight to some brown reeds and matted grass guarding a shoreline that dropped steeply to six or seven feet. I let the Biggs sink until it found the bottom, counting the entire way to gauge the time needed to reach a level inches above the dormant weed growth. Three or four quick six-inch strips, then several seconds of sinking, then repeat the process to imitate the emergence of the damsel nymphs. On the third sequence the line stopped and then ran away from me. Striking brought a rainbow into the air in a series of three quick jumps followed by several more. This was a motivated trout to be sure. The fish checked in at the eighteen-inch mark and maybe a pound-and-one-half. Another fifteen minutes produced two more and my friend paddled over.

"What the HELL are you using, Holt?"

"The Biggs Special. Want a couple?" I said, handing over a pair.

I took one more good trout before the window of activity closed, but that day converted one more to the congregation of the First Church of the Biggs Special.

Hallelujah and pass the mallard flank, brother.

Several guides were hanging out in the kitchen of Talia's lodge on the Bitterroot when I pulled in well after dark. They'd had a good day on a sweet river and were understandably happy about the shape of things at the moment. Cocktails and B.S. at twenty paces in the warm Montana air. I'd just finished banging out thousands of words on a guidebook project for a small publisher, work that more than likely would never see the light of print in my lifetime, but the upfront money paid some bills so I was not too upset. Late April was a time to chase turkeys and hunt trout east of the mountains. The guides had early morning clients to meet so they headed home well before midnight. Seeing them for even a few moments was enjoyable. Good friends made on the water are some of the best. Talia—and I burned the candle at both ends a bit as we caught up on events and made plans for the next day's departure. There was gear to pack—tents, sleeping bags, rods, reels, waders, cooking gear, coolers, food, booze, shotguns, shells, water jugs, cassettes, CDs, axes, saws, binoculars, tarps, and cameras plus all sorts of coats, gloves, sweaters, fishing shirts, and boots that we'd never use but somehow seemed at the time like dire necessities all the same. The next morning's shopping list was pared down to only three pages. As Robert Traver said, "Frugality is the fisherman's middle name."

Finally packed, we pulled out at the crack of nine o'clock and headed downriver along U.S. 93 toward Skalkaho Pass, a curvaceous road that wound through the Sapphire Mountains past the headwaters of Rock Creek, by Georgetown Lake, and downhill into the mining towns of Anaconda and Butte. First we stopped at guide Jack Mauer's house so Talia could pick up some Blue-Winged Olives Jack had tied. Wapati Flies is Mauer's way of augmenting his guiding income. He is known as the DI (drill instructor) among his peers for his no-nonsense approach to fishing and life in general. I'd floated with Jack before. We'd always managed to have lively discussions about politics, the environment, and NBA basketball. Both Mauer and I were Bulls fans and in a state of glory as a result of the team's recent NBA championship and soon-to-be-successful drive for another. We had both graduated from high school in 1969 and shared a somewhat similar mindset. Jack is a good man to have on your side. We chatted briefly, then struck out for the pass that wanders through some of the finest uncut forest in the Northwest. Pine-covered slopes stretch to the horizon in every direction giving way to rugged peaks, cliffs, and precipitous jumbles of eroded and shattered rock. Water runs out of the high country tumbling crystal pure toward the Bitterroot. The streams are filled with small cutthroat, bull trout (which you can no longer fish for west of the Continental Divide because of a drastic drop in their numbers due, in part, to habitat loss and poor management by various government bureaucracies), brook trout, mountain whitefish, rainbows, and even a brown or two. The Skalkaho drainage defines the concept of good country, and I hoped that plans by the Forest Service to offer the timber for clearcutting would be shot down in flames (the agency's main business is selling timber at a taxpayer loss so that private companies make a killing). The day was a classic. No clouds yet. Golden light moving toward bright white as the sun climbed higher in the sky. Nothing but blue sky and big-trout fantasies.

Our first objective was a small stream formed by a spring pouring out of the ground east of the town of Bridger just west of the arid Pryor Mountain country and some miles northeast of both the Beartooth Mountains and Yellowstone Park. Rumor, always rumor, suggested that the little stream was home to a population of fair-sized browns. We'd find out. The drive to Bridger was several hundred miles and we stopped at a small cafe for cheeseburgers, fries, and a beer. The road leading to the creek wound through parched grassland except where irrigation turned the countryside soft emerald. This looked like prime snake country, too, with piles of rock offering designer nesting sites for rattlesnakes. Places to be avoided. I'd never been bitten but a friend experienced in such matters advised that large adult snakes can control the amount of venom injected so the bite is less severe than that delivered by a young snake that shoots its full load into a victim's leg. Proving this observation was low on my addled list of priorities.

We first spied the creek flowing lazily beneath ochre cutbanks through posted ranch land. Posting of land has not been a major problem to date, but it's a practice that is growing yearly. Most people still offer access if you ask politely. Those who don't are just those who don't.

The creek was the location of a state fish hatchery and there was a small, level grassy spot with picnic tables and fire pits. The stream was fifteen feet wide at the most. Small browns rose eagerly to *Baetis* mayflies coming off the water. Talia, a hardened big-trout seeker, wanted to push on but I rigged a two-weight quickly and jumped in before he could point the Bronco back toward the dirt road. Fish averaging ten inches came eagerly to the fly. Rumor had them at about five pounds, but forty-five minutes of exceptionally skillful presentation on my part, one in three casts went where I planned, turned nothing larger than a foot. True, these were all nice, colorful browns and I would love to have this little stream burbling and splashing about in my back yard, but we needed a big-trout fix, badly. We pushed through the oil town of Billings, the flames of the gas burning off from the cracking process at the refineries lending a surreal glow to the night. The air smelled of petrochemicals. We crossed the Yellowstone River, climbed through the rimrocks on I-90, and rolled on south to Hardin, the Bighorn River, and Fay McCoy's Lariat Motel one day ahead of our reservations.

"I know how you fishermen are," Fay laughed when we checked in. She always seemed to have room for slightly crazed fly fishers. "See you in the morning," she said as we hauled some gear up to our rooms.

Not a big fan of motels, I find that every once in a while they are a worthwhile investment. I prefer camping but a hot shower and a warm bed are nice occasionally, as is cable TV. I flipped on MTV and tried to make sense of the station while sipping some bourbon and smoking a cigar from the Dominican Republic. Talia poked his head in the door and said, "Tomorrow the Horn, Holt. Later." Daylight would come soon so I went to bed.

We'd arranged a rental drift boat from Quill Gordon Fly Fishers in Fort Smith, the nexus for fly fishing on this famous stream. Gordon and June Rose run a friendly, no bullshit shop, an increasing rarity in a pursuit that is showing signs of caving in to hucksterism and avariciousness. When fly fishing "celebrities" start communicating through headsets and microphones while standing in artificial trout streams on the floors of neon-lit convention centers, something is seriously wrong. We are bombarded with messages saying that if we don't do the convention circuit we're out of the loop, whether one's a guide, writer, factory rep, or fly fisher. That is one loop I want no part of.

The first section of the river is known as the Upper 13 and receives by far the most pressure. There are two more sections below this baker's dozen miles that offer less crowded action for slightly larger fish that cruise around in smaller numbers. The top run, below Yellowtail Dam, is the most fertile and contains lots of good-sized trout that can be both easy and extremely difficult to catch depending on the weather, time of the year, and mood of the fish. I'd never rowed a drift boat before and since this was April the upper stretch river was somewhat empty. I volunteered to work the oars for the day, an offer Talia did not refuse. I'd get my licks in when we stopped along prime stretches of the float, especially across from the Gray Cliffs not far above the takeout.

The water was cold, clear, and moving at a decent pace. The day was cloudless again and temperatures were projected to flirt with the eighties. Not the best day for fishing but a glorious one in which to be alive. Talia began working a two-fly setup that had a Hare's Ear Nymph on the dropper and a fly I couldn't distinguish on the point. Within several minutes he turned a brown that was maybe fifteen inches, boating it quickly. The fish raced away on release. A good start. Another ninety minutes yielded four more fish—rainbows and browns to seventeen inches. Certainly not the wildly exaggerated accounts one reads in many of the hook-and-bullet magazines, but steady fishing nonetheless. At a stop along a wide, sweeping bend in the river that was in reality a huge spring creek, I took one fat rainbow on an Olive and then scared the hell out of the rest of the pod with a trademark water-slapping cast of forty feet.

Like riding a bicycle, you never forget the important skills in life.

We stopped for a leisurely lunch that we'd ordered from Fay's cafe, the legendary Chat N' Chew. Each box contained enough food for several NFL linemen. Staggering under a full load of roast beef sandwiches, chips, and donuts, I worked some line out to a few rising fish in a deep side channel. The first float was a good one and I nailed a brown of twenty inches. The ruckus put down the other fish. Oh well. We floated on and the fishing slowed in the afternoon heat. Talia switched to a Woolly Bugger and took several trout by buggering the banks and then working a wicked retrieve.

In truth, John is a skilled, predatory angler and buggering the banks is one of his most effective weapons. Woolly Buggers have also fooled more big trout for me than any other pattern. Give me a good supply of Buggers in black, olive, and brown, several shades of Elk Hair Caddis, the Biggs Special, a hopper pattern, some Hare's Ears, Royal Wulffs, and a small dry like the Blue-Winged Olive and I'm confident I can catch fish in most situations. Cut me off at the knees with just one pattern and I'll take the Bugger, with the Elk Hair coming in a close second. Most of us carry far too many patterns and spend far too much time and money buying and tying the latest gimmicks dreamed up by the previously mentioned "celebrities," whose main goal is not to improve our enjoyment of fly fishing but rather to fatten their wallets. This to me comes under the heading of greed and venality. As Talia can attest, I tend to get worked up over this sort of madness.

By the time we reached the Gray Cliffs the day had turned overcast and the humidity had risen significantly. We were tired from the long float but browns were working steadily as the *Baetis* emerged from the river taking long glides on the dark, glassy surface of the river in ideally damp conditions. We quickly dropped to 6X tippets and tied on #20 and 22 Blue-Winged Olives. I took several fish right away and missed as many more. All were browns from sixteen to twenty-two inches. Talia was taking fish in some healthy water below me. We fished like this for an hour before deciding to head to the takeout.

"Look at that damn tail, Holt," Talia exclaimed, pointing to a rocky point of a small island across the river.

"It must be a foot across," I added, staring at the biggest tail fin on a brown I'd ever seen. The trout was rooting around in the rocks kicking up nymphs and the angle of its feeding exposed the square fin. That brown was over ten pounds. Way over. We just looked at each other incredulously and laughed. Even as overcrowded and rowdy as it sometimes gets, the Horn is a fine piece of water. We beached the raft, unloaded our gear, ferried it to the waiting Bronco, and shed our waders. A couple of cold beers tasted great and we drove into Hardin for a pizza and a few icy pitchers. Good friends. Good water. Good weather. We were living now.

Morning again produced a clear sky and a forecast for temperatures above normal, nearly ninety, in the country off to the east where we were headed in search of turkeys in the ponderosa pine covered coulees and bluffs just above the Wyoming border. There is also some mar-

ginal fishing for browns in the Tongue River and supposedly some big rainbows and brook trout in isolated
ponds. The drive took us to the Little Bighorn Battlefield
near Crow Agency. Pulling in at the visitor center next to
the National Cemetery and its rows of white stone
crosses, the obelisk marking the remains of Custer and
his troops stood starkly atop the ridge where the men
had died. A sign on the asphalt path leading to the battle
site warned us to watch out for rattlesnakes. We did.
Standing on the ridge was a spooky feeling. It was like
the fighting had never stopped. The anger felt by the
tribes because of the government's harsh, violent policy
toward them and Custer's vigorous prosecution of his
orders, all of this rage was palpable as I stood on this
spot. So was what must have amounted to terror and a
sense of fatalism among the general's troops. There was
too much history to ignore. Hundreds of men had lost
their lives in one of humanity's most famous battles.

"Nice place to die. Look at the view," commented
Talia with a shudder. The Bighorn Mountains shimmered purple in the distance. Stone markers indicated
where the men had fallen. Several were at our feet, more
scattered down the slope to the Little Bighorn River, and
a number of others lying about in the thick green grass
over the hill. The strains of "Garryowen", an Irish drinking song favored by Custer, marched through my head. I
could visualize those soldiers fighting the good but futile
fight against tribes who were righteously taking out
their anger and grief on the most hated of all white men,
Custer. The markers behind us must have been soldiers
who tried to elude the Indians but had obviously been
tracked down and dropped along the narrow draw as the

battle neared its conclusion. Tough, lonely country and a rough way to go. There seemed nothing romantic about the Plains Indian Wars from any perspective. I was reminded of Cormac McCarthy's mind-blowing novel *Blood Meridian* about the Texas-Mexican frontier of 150 years ago. The real West wasn't John Wayne or *Lonesome Dove* or Kevin Costner's naive *Dances With Wolves*. It was blood and hideous, spontaneous violence and lonely death. It was starvation, brutal cold, unbearable heat, choking thirst, and 100 miles of the meanest road imaginable.

The two-lane highway took us east into a simmering sun through Busby and Lame Deer on the Northern Cheyenne Reservation as we streaked toward Ashland. The way into turkey land began as pavement and quickly degenerated into yellow-orange gravel and dirt. A cloud of dust rose in our wake, hanging in the dead still air for miles. This was my fourth year in this country during turkey season. Two of the first three had been successful and I knew exactly where the turkeys were. The sound of a twenty-five pound wild bird gobbling in the wilderness is far more majestic than you would think. We pulled into our dry camp on top of a coulee. Ponderosa shaded the spot. Turkeys gobbled in the distance and after each call coyotes howled not far behind.

We set up camp and Talia warned me off a clump of rocks that hid a king snake. His "snake eyes" were better than mine. Taking the turkeys the next morning was anticlimactic. Once you know where the birds are, the shooting involves rising before first light, getting in place, and waiting for the big birds to drop out of their roost tree with a sound like sacks of wet cement crashing on a city street. You pick the jake with the longest beard growing from its dark breast, then make a well-aimed head shot with a shotgun. Western hunting is far easier than that found in the East where the birds are more sophisticated and haven't been shot at as much.

After breakfast we drove some dirt roads to a trailhead leading to a lake that was reported to have brook trout. The mile walk in through grassy meadows filled with wildflowers and beneath tall pines was pleasurable. The air smelled of the needles, sweet grass, and flowers. The pond itself was a disappointment. Perhaps an acre of clear, spring-fed water with downed trees and some algae growth, it was obviously devoid of trout, sunfish, or minnows, but we cast for an hour anyway. Next stop was a pair of dredge ponds located below some tall bluffs to the east. These were also spring fed and also without trout. The few minnows here were intimidated by our small dries. We returned to camp, loaded our gear, and struck out for the Tongue some fifty miles to the south.

Gravel roads eventually gave way to a cracked narrow paved one that paralleled the river from above. We stopped at the sight of huge fish circling in the clear shallows.

"God-damned suckers, John. What have you gotten me into? Here are two fly fishermen miles from any trout," Talia said, grinning a vicious smile. I'd watch my back for now. When frightened never show fear in the face of the enemy. I cracked open a frosty beer and downed it in two gulps.

"Have faith Talia. We're not to the good water yet." We drove to the empty, primitive campground a mile below the dam spillway that held back the waters of the Tongue River Reservoir. The lake held many species of fish—carp, koi (dumped in by area residents), northerns, rainbows, walleyes, suckers, crappie, browns—you name it, but we were here to fish the river for browns.

The plunge pool below the dam cuts through layers of salmon, brown, gray, and yellow earth. Seams of black low-sulphur coal many feet thick are visible. This is prime coal country and some of the largest strip mines in the world operate near here. The ground rumbles with machines that move enough coal to fill a train car in a single scoop. Tires on the hauling trucks are as tall as two men. The scale of these operations is mammoth.

We cast into the brown, foaming water. I caught nothing. Talia defeated a pair of sauger, one of which sailed over my head upon release. Discouraged, we returned to camp for cocktails and grilled steak. Talia stayed by the fire while I went upriver to work a black Bugger. Now the river was alive with feeding fish. Browns? Suckers gulping air? Man-eating sauger? I worked the line under starlight, the streamer flying through the air with a cushioned "whoosh." Something attacked the Bugger and crashed about in the shallows. The beam of the flashlight revealed a brown of a couple of pounds. I caught one more, proving there was at least some truth to the rumor of good fish here. I'd be back in the fall to hunt sage grouse and cast to the browns.

All the same, we broke camp the next morning and drove three hundred miles to Armstrong Spring Creek in the Paradise Valley of the Yellowstone River. This was the first serious trip of the year in Montana for

both of us and a lot of pent-up energy from the winter was being burned off with road miles, a draining but necessary process for the more disciplined, difficult fishing that lay ahead this season. Actually it was a hell of a lot of fun rolling down the highway in search of whatever lay around the next curve. Kids at heart.

The wind was howling at Armstrong but we paid ten bucks for an afternoon's fishing. We were the only ones there. The fish were feeding, but the wind was so strong that setting the hook was next to impossible. The line bellied in the gale and pulled the fly from the trout. I took a brace of good browns on a Pheasant Tail above the Barnyard Bridge, line-striking on the take to cheat the wind. A half dozen more fish were missed. We headed up the valley to the old inn at Chico Hot Springs which features a couple of good bars, hot springs (a real surprise), comfortable rooms, old-fashioned ambiance, and an excellent restaurant. We ate lavishly and drank fine wine before retiring early. The next day would see us through Yellowstone Park and on to Slide Inn along the Madison.

We were through the Gardiner entrance to Yellowstone before eight. Climbing and twisting upward along the narrow road that followed the Gardner River (the town and river, for reasons clear to nobody I know, have different spellings) made us both wish that this were June and the park was open for fishing. Neither was the case, though. The Gardner is a wonderful little stream full of pocket water, riffles, and cascades that hold lots of rainbows and brook trout and some large browns up from the Yellowstone in the fall. The drive rolls past Mammoth Hot Springs, a huge terraced formation of white, yellow, and pink mineral deposits. The air was full of sulphur and steam as we passed. The upper Gardner flows through lush grassy meadows filled with browsing elk and buffalo. This is also a nice place to work light rods and delicate casts for smaller but discerning fish. The Gibbon also runs toward terrain of similar character and provides serene fishing for brooks, a few rainbows, and, below the falls, some browns that migrate up from the Madison. The last stretch of road in the park before the tourist town of West Yellowstone follows the Madison. Not being able to cast on these waters was painful. Fishing out of season crossed both our minds briefly; like hitting the crazy bone in an elbow, it hurt like hell but passed in an instant. The fires of 1988 had leveled a fair amount of the forest in the mountains and valleys we motored through, but the blackened, sooty land was showing strong signs of coming back. Neither of us had seen so many buffalo or elk as we did on this spring trip. All the weeping over the demise of the park from the late-summer conflagration was uninformed silliness—the wailings of those woefully naive concerning the way of the natural world. The consensus of those who fought the fires was that all of the efforts, with few exceptions like those around Old Faithful Lodge, were as effective as trying to put out a house fire with a bucket of water. The millions spent were more for PR. We continued on through West Yellowstone and past both Hebgen and Quake lakes before pulling off just below Slide Inn.

This stretch of the Madison, and the deep, wicked chutes above, holds some of the largest trout in the river, fish well over five pounds. Once again we had bluebird weather. The bright light would make the fishing tough. Both of us worked large stonefly nymphs through charging runs and swirling pockets. I took one small rainbow and Talia caught a pair of decent fish. Slow. A cloudy day would have been better.

Above Slide Inn the current is funneled into narrow rips that slam against the bends and bows in the gravel and boulder channel. To reach the trout holding in the undercuts you need weight, a lot of it, a stout leader, and a big stonefly nymph. Black, brown, gray—it doesn't matter. The fly is going past the fish at a pace approaching orbital velocity. This is in the angler's favor. The big trout do not have time to think about the possible food source. Is it real or is it Memorex? They must act quickly. Nothing about this fishing is pretty. A stiff eight-weight rod and a tippet testing over twelve pounds are useful, plus several twist-ons for sinkability, which I often attach to a dropper that is significantly weaker than the tippet in case the whole mess hangs up. That way, I'll lose the lead and not the #4 nymph. One other tip, passed on to me by John Randolph, editor of *Fly Fisherman*, is to use a Dai-Riki monofilament shooting line in place of your normal fly line. Its narrow diameter cuts through the boiling current with far less resistance than more conventional lines, reducing breakoffs to some extent. Details like this are the difference between landing an eight-pound rainbow and a depressing breakoff. One other point. Big fish, truly large trout, feed mainly in the dark or just before sunrise; when most of the so-called early risers hit the stream at sunup, the big fish are back in hiding. I am not a crack-of-dawn type of guy, as those who know me will attest, but for water that I know holds huge trout, I'll sacrifice personal comfort and rise before the sun is up. Fly fishers are a spartan bunch.

Along one very fast run, just south of Highway 287, I prepared to cast this ungainly rig. Before doing so, I planned my course of action looking for the least dangerous way through the jumble of rocks, limbs, and boulders downstream from me. Once the fish is on, you follow. Period. Casting the stonefly nymph well upstream and frantically mending in the slack, then digging the weighty setup out of the water and repeating the process becomes drudgery in a hurry. Maintaining concentration is difficult. On about the sixtieth drift the line halted. I reflexively lifted up and then the monofilament tore down through the torrent, sending a miniature burst of spray behind it like an invisible water ski slicing sharp curves outside a tow boat's wake. I ran after the berserk fish, banging my shins, and keeping up a steady flow of profanity. I tripped over a log and smashed my forearm, but the rod remained bent severely high above my head. The run calmed down after what felt like six compound leg fractures and the trout held at the edge of the current across the narrow chute. I crossed at a fast-water but passable ford twenty yards above, almost going under twice. On shore I gathered myself, my heart slamming against my ribs. The trout was still holding. I reeled in line as I approached cautiously, but the fish spooked, raced up and down along the current seam, then sounded. I could see a bright torpedo against the bottom through the blue-green water. I pulled and the rainbow came closer, then pumped and reeled until the fish was in the shallows, spent but resistant. I had no net and risked dropping the rod and pulling the fish to me by the line. A quick lunge secured it by the belly and tail. It was the biggest Madison River trout I'd caught—over twenty inches and easily more than five pounds, let's call it eight for the sake of feeling good. I was happy and took a few quick photos before turning the trout loose near the current. It struggled for a few seconds and I feared for its survival, but then the rainbow righted itself and shot from sight.

I've not been blessed with many fish like that one, but his kind are the reason Talia and I fished here even on a day we knew was all wrong. If big trout are of interest, you never pass up Slide Inn.

We'd been on the road for ten days and were beginning to burn out, but we stopped at Charlie Miller's place along the Ruby River. Charlie is an old friend of

Talia's from the Bitterroot and a recent friend of mine. He generously showed us some superb water on the Ruby that held browns, but the ninety-degree cloudless days worked against us again. We took a few medium-sized browns on the river and some smaller ones on spring creeks meandering through his property, but that was all. The highlight of the trip was when Charlie forced some people to the side of the road after they had pitched empty beer cans in the ditch. I think they understood Charlie's message.

The next day we passed through the upper Big Hole, flying through Jackson and Wisdom before dropping down into the Bitterroot via Lost Trail Pass. The East Fork was high but clear, as was the main river. There were still a few more days before the early heat would kick the runoff into high gear and blow out the rivers west of the Divide.

Saying goodbye to Talia, I pulled out of the Lodge. We'd meet up again on the Blackfeet Reservation in a few weeks. On the way north to Whitefish I stopped and watched a film crew making a fishing video on Nine Pipe Reservoir. Fly fishing videos as a whole have all the craft, art, and interest of a library filled with Cliff Notes. They are normally without substance, heart, soul, or conscience. In other words, they are a tangible metaphor for what is wrong with trout fishing in America. During the remaining hour or so of the drive home I worked out a screenplay for a video that I would pay a few dollars to see. No one will ever buy the concept, I'm sure, nor would I blow my own money on the story. Still ...

THE CHALLENGE OF TROPHY CARP
A Fly Fishing Video Screenplay Treatment

FADE IN
SCENE 1/Exterior—Rock & mud bank along Turtle Creek

Well-known fly fisher and pompous expert LaMarr North and veteran traveling angler Bobby Douglas stand next to a gray wooden row-boat. They hold fly rods while discussing the day's forthcoming adventure. The Rock River and several factory smokestacks of this downstate Wisconsin city dominate the background. Elevator Music's Greatest Hits is audible over the background noise of police and fire sirens and sporadic gunfire sounding in the distance. A crowd of locals throws rocks and heckles from a nearby bridge.

BOBBY (*with obvious smarmy enthusiasm*)
Ignore them. They're just jealous because they won't be fishing with us today. Well, LaMarr, this is the water I've been telling you about all winter. The Rock is some of the finest big-carp turf in the world. I mean the fish are hot in these parts. And having the chance to teach you the tricks of the chase and share the excitement of this fishing is a thrill of a lifetime, at least mine.

LAMARR (*bored and not quite with the program*)
Hey! That clown over there just threw a piece of raw meat at me. Your mother, too, fella. Where in the hell is that awful sound coming from?

BOBBY

You mean all the sirens?

LAMARR

No! That damn awful music. God! How can you put up with that brain-dead noise? Here's your meat back, sucker. Go steal a Weber... and the horse you rode in on, buddy.

BOBBY

Come on, forget about them. The music is part of the video, LaMarr. We couldn't possibly hope to sell this stuff to the fly fishing public without this music. I mean for $89.95 we have to make it look like we're giving them something. And you'll get so you don't hear it after a while, just like when you're actually watching one of our Crashing Boar fishing videos in your very own living room.

LAMARR

In your dreams, buddy. Why don't you just dub the crap back at the studio? How 'bout givin' them a quart of Johnny Walker Black instead of that lame music. If they're gonna watch this junk, they'll need a bottle. You'll still make a bundle. And by the way, you better hope that check you sent me clears the bank.

BOBBY

Come on, LaMarr, we're here to enjoy ourselves. Besides, studio dubbing might lend an air of professionalism to the tape. No one in this field is ready to try that, yet. Let's go cast to one of North America's finest game fish.

LAMARR

You got Atlantic salmon here? I thought we were going to throw whiskey doughballs at some goddamn carp.

BOBBY

No salmon. Mighty carp, though, Lamarr, and watch the language. Too much editing ruins the continuity of even the best fly fishing video.

LAMARR

Continuity my ass. You ever see anyone after they watched one of these tragedies? Their eyes look like a Thorazine overdose. Sort of how I plan to be before much longer. Language. Editing. $3,000 bucks to spend in two days in southern Wisconsin fishin' for carp of all goddamned things. Bad enough my publisher screwed me on the book royalties, now I got to fish for stinking carp. I'm gettin' the hell out of here and find a real job. Maybe wear a paper hat and hustle Big Macs.

BOBBY

Come on LaMarr. Get in the boat here and Let's Go Fishin!

SCENE 2—Moving onto the river and slowly downstream.

LaMarr stumbles into the front seat of the boat, dropping a pint of bourbon as he leans over the gunwale to look into the water. More swearing, but Bobby manages to rig a doughball onto LaMarr's hook and finally gets him casting along a deep oily run.

BOBBY

Now we're living, eh LaMarr?

LAMARR

You haven't had much of a life, have you Bobby boy? God, what's that awful smell and Christ, these are the heaviest damn life jackets I've ever worn.

BOBBY

That's from the cheese factory right over there. We're using their cheddar for the doughballs. These aren't life jackets. They're flack jackets just in case, you know, if there's any gunfire.

LAMARR

Gunfire? What the hell's going on here? I thought we were carp fishing and making a video to sell to the yuppy mooches. You didn't say anything about gunplay.

BOBBY

Times are tough, LaMarr, and this is a factory town experiencing layoffs. Crime is up and the cops are jumpy. Never hurts to be safe.

LAMARR

You mean you're actually going to encourage people to come here and fling rotten food at carp? They would get their heads blown off. And I thought selling the same article to six magazines was bad. Whatever happened to the bamboo rod days?

BOBBY (*exasperated*)

Come on LaMarr. You want the back-end of your fee. Shut up and catch a carp. Maybe we can salvage something. And could you double haul next time. Without that, we'll have to drop the price down to $49.95. Got to have the double haul. The viewers like that.

LAMARR (*takes a healthy pull from the pint and belches*)

Whatever you say Captain. So I just drift the bait on the bottom here and a carp will hit the thing?

BOBBY (*showing a toothy smile*)
Now you're catching on LaMarr. We'll film you playing the fish from that boat over there. We'll do all the
work. Land the fish and we'll stick a big tarpon fly in
its mouth and shoot that for the closeup and release.
If we can't tag a carp, I've got this bent coat hanger
for you to reel in. Fights just like the real thing.
Learned that trick from a guy who does a show out
West.

LAMARR
When did you ever taste the real thing, Bobby Baby?
What a business, and people actually buy this crap. Those
guys in that boat over there friends of yours?

BOBBY
No. Why?

LAMARR (*pointing to the boat*)
'Cause they're taking in water and I wouldn't swim in
this crud for love nor money.

BOBBY
The film crew has been through worse. Don't worry. The
camera's insured and waterproof. Isn't that right, Wink?

*SCENE 3—Large eddy just above four-lane
bridge in city*

*After four hours of no action, LaMarr finally
hooks a good carp and the camera crew closes in
for action footage. Bobby attempts a play-by-
play after beaching boat on top of half-sub-
merged, rusted-out Plymouth Roadrunner. Three
squad cars, lights flashing, sirens whooping,*

corner a powder-blue Ford Torino being used as a getaway car by two armed men who apparently just robbed a local bank.

LAMARR (*fighting the carp, while nervously glancing up over his shoulder at the mayhem taking place on the bridge*) What in God's name is going on up there, Bobby Blue? Damn strong carp, though. I'll give you that much.

BOBBY (*moves in with net and large orange fly*) Keep it up LaMarr. Way to palm that reel. Nice job of keeping that pig off balance by shifting that rod tip. Boys, move below and get both LaMarr and the squad cars. I can feel it. Bigtime catalog sales. And we'll pump this number through every fly shop in West Yellowstone. That ranchette on the Boulder River is mine. Come LaMarr. Bring that carp to Papa. Guys, did you get that one bum taking it in the face up on the bridge? Shotgun sure makes a mess. You did? Fantastic! We're in like gold.

LAMARR (*fighting the carp as a bullet knocks him face forward into the river next to a bloated catfish*) Dammit... What in the hell... Bobby Bubba, I've been hit. Help me. Get the bourbon. Net the carp. Sign the check. There's a dead body next to me.

SCENE 4 —Cut to the bridge where cops surround shot-up robbers.

COP #1

Jesus! Look at that fool lying in the water next to that dead fish. Who shot him?

COP #2

I did. I got carried away and look at that red-nosed son-of-a-bitch. He needed shooting.

COP #1

Yeh. He is an ugly piece of work. Sort of like these two bums. Where's that little creep photographer from the paper, anyway?

SCENE 5—Pan back to Bobby netting LaMarr's carp.

BOBBY (*really grinning now*)

What a shot...

LAMARR (*lying on his back near shore*)

No shit.

BOBBY (*quickly unhooking doughball and inserting fly*)

Get a close up. No. Forget LaMarr. There. Tight on the fly. Now on the fish as he swims away. Great. You're a pro LaMarr. Quick guys, get him kneeling. What a mood. No LaMarr. Not the pint. Not now. You got enough? Good. We can cut and paste this one for all it's worth.

LAMARR (*taking a healthy blast*)

Here's to you Bobby my man. Damn flack jacket saved my life. I can market these hummers. Damn fine carp, too. Fought like a Grouper every inch of the way. Lousy whiskey, though. I really must find a real job. Hey Bobby Bomber, is there a K-Mart in town?

BOBBY (*arm-in-arm with LaMarr*)

Come on my friend, let's go have one on the company. Secure the tape, guys. Then meet us at the Zoo Gardens for boilermakers and fried catfish.

SCENE 6 —Pan of city skyline as sun disappears behind a yellow cloud of smoke, then pan downstream on the Rock River.

Police and ambulance sirens are heard fading in the distance. Happy fishing small talk and the sound of wadered feet sliding on greasy rock are also heard off camera. The carp is seen floating belly up beneath the bridge as the Elevator Music version of the Rolling Stones' "Sympathy for the Devil" comes up.

LAMARR

Can I have my check now, Bobby buddy?

BOBBY

Let's have a few of those drinks first, then we'll do business. Let's savor the moment. Fishing like this just doesn't happen every day, right LaMarr? This one's going to retail for $109.95, easy.

LAMARR

I want my check now Bobby …

I was still trying to find someone to film the screenplay some days later when a friend drove up in his battered pickup truck, a small, sky-blue Ford that was a true fishing rig. Ragged, rusting body, camper shell with broken windows, noisy muffler getting louder by the day, capricious starter. A fine outfit. Would I like to head over to the Thompson River for some fishing? Sure. The video concept was dead in the water. That was plain to see, though I still hadn't heard back from Redford.

The Thompson is a beautiful little river west of Missoula and south of Libby twenty mountainous miles from Idaho. The river is fertile, perhaps more so than Rock Creek. Turn over any rock and bunches of mayfly and stonefly nymphs along with caddisfly larvae crawl for darkness. The water is clean, filled with nutrients, and stays cool enough in the summer to support many more trout than it currently does. There are rainbows, cutthroat, brook trout, bull trout, mountain whitefish, and some huge browns up for spawning in the fall. The only problem is that the Department of Fish, Wildlife and Parks caved into a concerted phone and letter campaign conducted with brutal efficiency by the meat mongering bait fishing populace from nearby Thompson Falls. This led to a lifting of catch-and-release regulations on seventeen miles of some of the prettiest trout water anywhere. This amounts to a policy of giving in to whatever segment of the angling public that whines the loudest. Never mind what is right or in the best interests of the stream and the fish. I could visualize the process down at headquarters.

"Boy, we got a bunch of letters from those guys in Thompson Falls screaming about catch-and-release," exclaims one department employee. There is sweat beading on his forehead. "Man they're pissed about not getting to keep the big fish over there."

"Tell me about it. You should have heard the call I got from a guy who says he's logged the woods over there all his life and he never had anyone tell him he couldn't kill all the fish he wanted whenever he wanted," adds another employee with a bemused and slightly rattled expression. "Sure wouldn't want to cross that one. Let's pull the catch-and-release regs."

"I'm with you," the first chimes in. "Those simpering, weak-tit fly fishing clowns won't do much anyway."

"You got that right. We've got them B.S.'d three ways from Sunday."

And the deed is done and a decent piece of water gets hammered in the name of expediency. Still, the river is fun to fish, easily accessible by gravel roads, and a few good trout hang out in the deep pools and along the bottoms of slick runs. Rarely exceeding sixty feet in width, the Thompson is easy to wade with a modicum of prudence, and it's easy enough to fish. The fish are where they should be.

The day was already hot, like so many this spring, when we pulled the truck off the road above a series of chutes, cascades, riffles, runs, and pools. We'd catch fish here but they'd average less than a foot when they should have run in the fifteen- to seventeen-inch range with consistency. While rigging up we watched a pair of bait fishers derrick a couple of fat trout out of a dark hole. One a brookie, the other a rainbow. Both a couple of pounds. The sound of the trout's heads being thwacked on heartless rock sounded sick, perverted on this beautiful May morning. Maybe it is time for fly fishers to play the department's ugly little "raise some hell to get what you want" game.

My friend went upstream to work a series of pockets and small falls with a large pattern, the Ugly Bitch, that looked like a Girdle Bug. I went downstream with high hopes for a yellow-orange Stimulator that I imagined might drum up some action based on a few yellow stones and even fewer salmonflies I saw helicoptering above the water. The salmonfly hatch is famous (infamous?) from the Madison to the Big Hole to Rock Creek. The Thompson has a good hatch also, but we appeared to be ahead of the action which kicks off several weeks before that on the more famous waters. There were only a few dried exoskeletons on the rocks near the river. Either that or this was an off year.

A clear run along the near bank looked promising, its surface braided and scrambled by large rocks along the streambed. Trout were rising to both caddis and several species of stoneflies, one a #14, quite small for this burly insect family. The Stimulator rode nicely on the current like a horny teenager on the prowl in his flashy convertible. The bug was sucked in by a greedy little rainbow that leaped and shimmied its way to hand. Ten inches. Silvery with a clear lateral red band. A typical, these days anyway, Thompson River rainbow. I took a few more from the stretch with easy, short upstream reach casts. The largest fish was a foot long. Farther down where a boulder cut the flow, the fly was nailed as soon as it swung by the midstream side. The fish flashed in the crisp light and ran for the far shore. Checking it was no problem even with a light tippet and a three-weight. A couple of brief sprints downstream and the trout gave up. A touch larger this time, a plump fourteen inches. Nice.

A quarter mile of this fishing turned nearly twenty trout in the same range. Two were brooks and one was a mountain whitefish, the ubiquitous native of the northern Rockies. Even in streams like the Jefferson they outnumber trout by a ratio of three or four to one. Fly fishers as a whole hate the species, but I'm glad they're around. They are natives, after all, and they fight well and taste even better when smoked. I'd rather catch trout, to be sure, but I'm not of the pious school that casually flings the poor fish far into the woods with disdain. That effort should be reserved for those in the Department of Fish, Wildlife and Parks who eliminate catch-and-release regulations. Although some of the best fisheries' biologists in the world toil in the agency, they are hamstrung by career bureaucrats fearful to the point of raging paranoia about losing their jobs.

It is difficult not to be cynical when fishing the Thompson, even with the action we were having this day. Four years of enforced catch-and-release or even slot limits would turn this stream and many others into world-class fisheries.

"Holt. You're swearing out loud again. Let it go."

My friend figured out what I was thinking. Easy enough to do. He's active in Trout Unlimited and has done as much as anyone for the fishing in the state, but even he, in moments of infrequent lucidity and candor, admits the fight might be futile.

"How'd you do?" I asked.

"I caught two trout on the Ugly Bitch that made my day. Both were sixteen inches," he grinned.

That made sense. The better trout would be holding undercover in the depths. My dry fly was taking the smaller fish feeding blissfully at the zenith of their carefree childhoods. My biggest trout had come from the security offered by the boulder.

We worked other places along the river with similar results, plenty of small fish on top and one or two fat ones on the bottom. On the drive upriver we pulled over to cast a few minutes on a small tributary that tumbled out of a narrow, rocky canyon. This was classic pocket pool holding water never more than twenty feet wide. A #16 Royal Wulff took brook and cutthroat trout on almost every short cast. A quick flick of the line, a foot or two of drift, and a few wild, eager fish would race for the privilege of tagging the fly. Three fish per hole was tops. The little buggers wised up after that. No matter. Five steps and there was another pocket to be picked. I lost track of time and the number of fish caught and released. This would be a perfect place to pitch a small camp and eat some pan-sized trout rolled in corn meal, salted and peppered, and fried in bacon grease. A squeeze of lemon and you were home. I made a note of a dandy spot overlooking the stream on a rock outcropping covered in thick moss and a deep carpet of pine needles.

Walking back through the woods the dryness of the duff was frightening. Moisture was scarce this year and without a lot of rain soon, the fire season would be a vicious, choking, eye-burning, forest-destroying hell. The ground crunched dryly under foot. Green grasses were already fading to yellow. Not good. Through the trees I spotted the road and the truck, so I dropped down to the stream where I was greeted by a most curious sight. Beyond the rectangular view afforded beneath the road's wooden bridge I spotted my friend, at least his hair and eyes. The rest of him was submerged. He was either exhibiting extreme stealth or the stream had a few deep-water surprises. The latter proved to be the case.

"Water's cold," he observed.

"I can see that." We drove home after breaking down our rods and changing clothes. It had been a good day despite the gloomy ruminations on trout management.

A float down one of the most beautiful canyons in the West is an invigorating experience unless the weather decides to play games. That's what happened to us on a late spring trip down this undisciplined, wild stream. In the mountains and adjacent high plains of Montana, spring is rarely a sure thing until maybe mid-June, if then. An unpredictable climate is part of the routine in this territory. The wind and rain made life tough on the river at times. The vertiginous upper ledges and overhangs a thousand feet above the water moved in and out of sight as swirling sheets of dark mist dropped in ragged layers from a mean late spring storm spawned in the heart of the Pacific. The sun made periodic appearances with all the enthusiasm of someone caught in the grip of a desperate Monday morning hangover. There were eight of us paired on four rafts for this sixty-mile drift down central Montana's Smith River, one of the premier trips in the Rockies, but snowmelt and heavy precipitation had turned the water yellow-brown with clarity measured in inches instead of feet. The fishing for browns and rainbow was slow, to be generous. We called it a very good day if we took several trout each.

So why had the voyage not turned into a disaster riddled with foul tempers and ugly remarks? Simple. Everyone here was an experienced fisherman and outdoorsman. We all knew that you take the good with the bad and you do your damnedest to make the bad enjoyable. The country was fantastic even in its often obscured state. The food was excellent. As was the wine, whiskey, and beer. The conversation around evening fires was spirited if not tilted toward the hyperbolic, and the few trout we caught were fat, healthy fish. I'd rather float a river and cast a line in the drizzle than sit behind a desk any day.

My friend, novelist Bob Jones, and his friend, photographer Bill Eppridge, were also along, as were guides Jack Mauer, Gary Throckmorton, Eric Shores, and Talia. A good crew.

I drew Mauer—or he drew me—and the first day began in high style with Jack telling me to not throw any refuse in the river and my responding that I'd been fighting a slightly crazed environmental battle for years. We came to an eye-to-eye understanding that was anything but contentious. In the first mile of the float it became apparent that fishing dries was fruitless so we decided to work sink-tip lines. Jack offered to pull over to allow me to change spools safely but I said that there was no need and promptly rolled the spare off the tube of the raft into the water. Jack looked at me with an expression that said, "I hope the next four days are not more of the same." Despite that beginning, Jack and I shared many hours of intense, enjoyable conversation about the state of the world and the NBA over the ensuing ninety-six hours.

We covered slightly over fifteen miles per day for each of the four days we were on the river. By the time we reached camp, a warm fire, a few drinks, a good meal, and a few more drinks took on shadings of pampered elegance. Talia, who loves to cook, bombarded us with fresh salads, hot rolls, buffalo steaks, grilled roast chicken, pork chops, and assorted snacks. We were in no danger of starving.

When eight adventurous adult men escape the confines of society and all its noisome restrictions, life becomes relaxed. The first night several of us stood on the edge of one beached raft casting to rising browns in the dark, guided only by a flashlight. We caught nothing but the activity was still good sport. Eppridge was a source of constant interest. Most photographers are gadget freaks; Eppridge has elevated it to a high art. His tools, lenses, film, rods, reels, camera bodies, and curious clothing (including a unique flapped hat) inspire amazement. At a hardware store in White Sulphur Springs he bought eight packages of twist-ons, enough to take a sane fly fisher into the next century. As we were leaving the store he fixed me with an earnest look and asked if he should run back in and grab a few more packages. Why not. They could always double as an anchor.

On the third day of the float I switched with Talia so that he and Jack could discuss some future fishing business. Throckmorton and I lagged well behind the other three rafts. We took the casual approach, sipping beer and discussing relevant topics that included nesting geese and aliens we have known (a not uncommon subject in Montana). Every now and then I would launch an olive Woolly Bugger bank-tight and make a sincere attempt at a lifelike retrieve. Where the others in our group suffered through a tough day, we managed to take over a half dozen browns, each a good fish. We were secure in the belief that we knew where to pick our spots. The best fish of the day came as we idled past a partially submerged grassy bank. From upstream I noticed a small eddy tight to shore.

"I think I'll pop one in here for the hell of it Terry."

"Good idea, but don't spill your beer."

The cast came in just above the swirl and the first strip was stopped dead and then a big brown boiled in the grass. The fish stayed tight and ripped its head back and forth, thrashing its body like a python trying to crush a small rodent. Terry skillfully slammed the raft ashore just below the trout and grabbed the net. Several tense moments later and the trout was ours. Twenty-three or twenty-four inches and heavy. We were quite pleased with ourselves and let the rest of the countryside know it. In the photos we took then, I look like I believed I was still in the running with DeNiro for the lead in *Cape Fear*—an ugly sight, salvaged only by the huge brown trout bulging in my hands. A good fish for the Smith or any other river. That was a satisfying day. The best, from a fishing perspective, on the trip.

We were on the river at this time of the year because being here earlier could mean encountering hurricane-driven sleet, snow, and bitter cold. Any later and we would have to contend with a flotilla of rafts, canoes, kayaks, inner tubes, and other craft that would destroy the isolated aesthetic of the trip. The Smith, like many rivers, suffers from overuse. Doug Habermann, one of the many good guys at the MDFWP (and there are quite a few), is in charge of controlling the onslaught of floaters as well as managing the often overcrowded campsites. Fights are not uncommon near the end of the day as rafters attempt to secure prime locations. Somehow chains and knives flashing beneath the stony silence of the ancient rock walls seem grossly out of place. Habermann has also been working with a variety of groups—floaters, fly fishers, guides, outfitters, and other sportsmen to hammer out regulations that will ameliorate the overcrowding without denying access to user groups. It is a difficult task that is proceeding surprisingly well. There is hope that the new Smith River regulations can serve as a model for other rivers like the Green, Bighorn, and Salmon, though each has their own unique set of problems.

By the end of June water levels are far too low to float the river. Dragging a raft over the miles of shallows is possible but not recommended for either floaters or craft. With the freshets of fall the water rises and the Smith is accessible once again. October can be chilly, but the brown trout are on the move and the crowds are long since gone.

By day four the river was basically a roiling sea of mud and debris. Fishing was futile but we cast anyway. While drowning a black Bugger in the heart of the maelstrom, not paying the slightest attention to the drift, the rod bent sharply to the water and the line ran upstream before the tippet snapped. Only a very large trout takes a fly in such heavy, discolored water and runs as powerfully upstream as this one did. I noticed Bob looking at me with a wry smile from his raft downstream. He knew what had just happened.

We passed a small flow known as Hound Creek that came in from the south not far above the takeout. The land is posted and even if it were not, the abundant population of rattlesnakes precludes fishing. Too bad since the water is full of brown trout.

Great Falls is only minutes from the landing and we soon saw jets streaking above. Helicopters from a nearby Air Force base shattered the silence. We were out of the wilderness. I looked at Mauer and he shrugged. The trip was over, except for the fact that the people running the shuttle had failed to ferry Throckmorton's rig and he had a flight to Alaska the next day. As it was, Jones, Eppridge and I ran out of gas, but a friendly rancher was finally rousted and we rolled into Cascade to top off the tank. On the trip back to White Sulphur Springs we crossed the Little Belt Mountains where a heavy storm dumped a foot of snow on the country and turned the road treacherous. Prior to returning to Whitefish the next morning we did some sedate carousing at a few bars in town. I was ready for home the next day.

The heat of this unusual spring carried through into June. The rivers in my country were blown out with spring runoff. The North Fork of the Flathead was a raging, swirling torrent of mud, glacial flour, deadfalls spinning like twigs in the gigantic whirlpools, and carcasses of deer, elk, and lesser mammals that succumbed to winter. Boulders the size of pickup trucks driven by unrelenting current collided with each other, the sound of the explosions reverberating through the ground and cracking the air with loud "crumps." Pieces of rock blasted through the surface. The Middle and South forks were the same. So was the main river along with the Swan, Stillwater, Whitefish, and Tobacco rivers, as were all of their tributaries. There would be no fishing here for a few weeks. The high country lakes were still buried under melting ice and snow. Time to head over Marias Pass and fish the Blackfeet Reservation.

Talia pulled into the driveway in the Bronco. The back of the rig was partially filled but we managed to cram my float tube, rods, cooler, and duffel bags in somewhere. I kissed Lynda, Jack, Elizabeth, and Rachel goodbye and we were off. I'm blessed with an understanding and patient family.

"My river is blown out and so is Rock Creek, the upper Clark Fork, and the Blackfoot," said Talia. "The weather forecast says hot and dry for the next week. We're in luck Holt," he grinned.

"Don't forget the wind," I cautioned.

"Nothing can be worse than the last two springs we had over there."

He was probably right. The first year four of us including Charlie Miller fished four long, windy, cold days in early May. We caught fewer than ten fish between us. That was a tough trip, but we avoided any fistfights and had a good time in spite of the weather. The second year Talia and I went it alone staying in East Glacier at a quiet collection of whitewashed cabins, an ideal place to work the Reservation. Again, wind disrupted the fishing. One afternoon turned so rough, we barely made it back to shore. My float tube was hurled by the storm toward Great Falls before being pinned to the side of the Bronco. The wind blew so hard that the surface of the lake, which is located along the edge of the Rocky Mountain Front, was slammed down flat. Heavy air jet-streaming over the Rockies poured through narrow gaps in the serrated range above us. Devil winds of white spray skittered across the lake's dark surface bouncing off each other like a wild, unfettered pinball game. We hunkered down in our tubes waiting for the blowout to pass. We learned later that gusts of 100 mph had been recorded in the region. Ideal fishing conditions for the criminally insane.

The only way we took trout was to rise at three-thirty in the morning after getting to bed around one. Days are long in May this far north. We'd race along the eastern edge of Glacier Park to the water, rig up, and start fishing at five. By seven-thirty the wind was upon us, but we did take some big rainbows. I hit one that went over twenty-eight inches and fought like a dog, but it was a ten-pounder and those are rare. On the last morning Talia took a number of trout, one of eight pounds, on the nymph from a quiet bay. So once again we were happy. Hardcore fly fishers are an easily amused collection of social flotsam, a proud and unjustly ma-ligned segment of the population. In a civilized world we'd be venerated as untamed artists working with graphite and bright lines. Life is often unfair.

This year we figured the weather would have calmed to more civilized proportions by mid-June. Driv-ing along U.S. 2 the sight of water pouring out of the mountains, flying over the edge of rock chutes, and roaring along narrow streambeds was constant. The pines were flushing bright green, especially the larch which had recently popped their buds at this altitude. The countryside was alive. We'd either calculated correctly or lucked out. Conditions were ideal: balmy with some wind by afternoon, but only to 20 or 30 mph, supreme calmness on the Reservation.

We checked in at the same place in East Glacier, unloaded gear, and headed for the Lake of Many Hurricanes. The wind was working as we lurched along the two-lane path to the water. Rigging up I noticed a band of Indian ponies on a distant hill. The wandering hills were bright green studded with wildflowers. The mountains were purple with white peaks except where avalanches had left rough scars exposing tan and slate gray rock. This was wild country at its best and I hoped that a proposed oil well would be kicked back to the dark halls of corporate greed where it belonged. The project would ruin this land. Rumor indicated that clandestine machinations were already underway to sabotage the project with guns and dynamite if the Bureau of Land Management and the Forest Service's approval of this proposed indecency held up in federal court. I'd be glad to help in any way possible.

The far shore featured some tall gravel cutbanks that gave way to an extended cobble shore. This was a good place to probe for rainbows. Paddling over took about fifteen minutes and I trolled a Biggs Special behind me. Nearly there, a trout took me by surprise, popping the fly and then running and leaping in high agitation sharply away from me before turning and charging my legs. Loose line was everywhere. The fish was winning this one. The rainbow spooked at the sight of my fins, tearing by at Mach I on the right. The hook still held. I stripped in line frantically to take up slack. The trout broke the surface shaking its head while still rushing away. Soon it was on the reel and I had the grand illusion of being in control of the situation, a fallacy that was dramatically revealed when the fish arced against the sky looking like it had been pitched above the water by an unseen hand, reminiscent of those phony "Bass-n-Heat" lure commercials that pepper the likes of "Jimmy Bill Bob's Flippin' For Hawgs" TV shows that run before the religious programming on Sunday mornings. The rainbow crashed back to the water, snapping the leader as it went. The fight was over and I was rattled as usual, but at least the trout had killed the dead time between put-in and reaching the cutbanks.

The wind was cut by the land and the relative stillness was loud. Casting was easy. Sixty feet right onto the sandy beach and then slow, halting strips back to the tube. The false spawn of June, a time when the rainbows go through the ritual of procreation without tangible result, was over. Trout populations on the Reservation are introduced and are not self-sustaining. Streams providing spawning sites are scarce. This is dry country. Upwelling springs provide most of the water in this area. The rainbow mules were in the shallows searching for forage fish, exposed nymphs, and leeches. The damsel imitation I was casting could pass for any of these with some imagination on the trout's part. There were always fish along here and I expected one right away. I was disappointed, not just on the initial presentation but for several dozen more. The sound of wind-rustled grass and stomping horse hooves drifted over my head as it swept off the rise above like a fighter catapulting from an aircraft carrier into a sea breeze.

The number of memorable trout I've taken absentmindedly, without artifice or skill, is astonishing. Trout over twenty inches or less than a foot, but big for a certain piece of water, have snapped at my fly when I'm turning to trudge off dejectedly to the next promising bend in a creek or when I'm fiddling with a zipper on my vest while the fly sinks to the bottom of a lake. This happens with such frequency that the first person who is able to explain the phenomenon in workable prose would either make a million dollars or be hung by the self-anointed "experts" fearing for the health of their heavy-handed over-hyped careers dedicated to the promulgation of extraneous information. The book would find a place in my library.

This was such an occasion. I was attempting to light a dark-wrappered (oscuro) Connecticut-made throwaway cigar. Stick matches were smoldering and fuming on my chest, in my lap, and in my hands when the rod was nearly pulled free of the Velcro retaining straps on the tube. I grabbed it with both hands above the reel as line tore through the guides, the drag making wonderful screeching noises. The rainbow charged back and forth near shore, its head and dorsal and tail fins cutting the water. I worked the flippers to face the direction of the trout as it tail-walked across the top of the lake heading, it seemed, toward the mountains looming above a grove of rustling aspens in the west. The rainbow stopped, then took off again ripping more line free as the rod bent and jerked to a submarine rhythm filled with jazz-like holes and pauses. Ornette Coleman salmonid style. Paddling toward the center of the lake, the trout holding onto the distance it had gained, offered a larger playing field. There were no weeds and the water was deep. This one could run all he wanted. With an eight-weight rod and 250 yards of backing I was in control as long as the five-pound tippet held and the clinch knot didn't slip. Neither the trout nor I knew it at the time, but the fight was over aside from some stubborn head shakes, deep divings, long-distance runs, and impressive, crashing leaps. This smaller trout had been a much more sporting fish than the ten-pounder of last year. There was no way the net attached to a ring on the tube could contain the fish, so I grabbed it by the tail as the tippet snapped with a shake of the rainbow's head.

"Gotcha, dammit."

The fish felt chilled, slippery, firm. It measured twenty-five inches and was thick and deep. There was plenty of crimson on the gill plates and along the flanks. The back was aquamarine and the rest of the body was stone-cold silver with black spots. This one I really wanted to kill for reasons I could only guess at, but my hand, with an ethical mind of its own, released its grip and the fish dropped from view. Determining the length of the catch is a way to prolong the brief contact and to rein in my active imagination. I'm embarrassed at the number of sixteen- and seventeen-inch fish I've called twenty inchers down the years. A trout over twenty inches is a different breed of fish. It more often eats bigger prey and its jaw structure shows this change of habit. A fish over two feet has taken this process to its predatorial conclusion. These trout live to eat other fish. That is why I'm always amazed and shocked when one of these giants takes a #10 damsel nymph or, stranger still, a #24 Trico. What in the hell is going on here? These are moments when I realize how little I really understand about my quarry and I'm thankful. To some extent ignorance really is bliss. Too much knowledge, assumed or otherwise, tears the soul out of natural mystery and wonder, the magic, that draws me to rivers and lakes. I don't want to read 100,000 words on emergers. Give me a small box of soft-hackled flies and I'll wing it.

"Nice trout, Holt," Talia offered while playing a leaper of his own. "This sure beats last year out here."

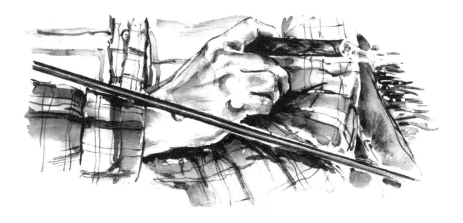

Yes it does, I thought, as the cigar finally caught despite being wet in spots from the spray of the last fish. I paddled around puffing on it and sipping a beer pulled from one of the float tube's many pockets. Marvelous devices, absolutely marvelous. I felt like venerable royalty afloat in a private world. Talia was quiet but grinning to my right. Clouds swirled among the peaks and the sun dripped honeydew sunlight over the lake.

"Holt, you're a waxing sentimental," boomed an unfamiliar voice in my head.

"Who said that?"

"I did."

"Who?"

I must be losing my mind, I thought, and a deep voice from within said, "you don't really want to know that, do you?" I finished the cigar and beer and went back to fishing. Talk about getting goofy in the wilds.

The weather and the fish held for the four days we fished the Reservation. We took big brookies from an isolated lake up in the foothills, browns and rainbows from a huge body of water near Canada, more rainbows on the breezy lake, and still more rainbows from a middle-of-nowhere pond out on the prairie. The fishing was as steady and exciting as any I'd ever experienced over the years on the Blackfeet. There was dry fly action in the stillness of sunrise, and streamers took fish any-time, as did nymphs and soft hackles. We saw few other anglers during the trip. Most of them concentrated their efforts on better-known waters or began fishing long after we'd left. A very general rule of thumb for the Reservation is that one day in three is unfishable due to wind and one day in ten has flat out superb fishing. Perhaps the same held true for years. One in ten. The coming months would tell whether or not this season was to be one of the magic few.

S U M M E R

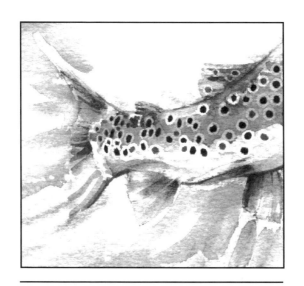

THE FEVER
BURNS
WHITE HOT

THE FEVER
BURNS
WHITE HOT

With runoff still raging full tilt in mid-June, a planned trip to Iceland seemed perfectly timed. Tony Acerrano, a field editor for *Sports Afield* and an old friend, and I were heading for that North Atlantic island as summer officially arrived. We met in Manhattan, swilled a few martinis, boarded a jet to soar over Newfoundland and the tip of Greenland, and dropped down into the airport at Keflavik, a six-hour hop. The flight was uneventful and we arrived in Reykjavik after a forty-minute bus ride. We hooked up with our Icelandic guides the next morning in the main lobby of the Hotel Saga and struck out for the interior in a pair of four-wheel-drive rigs. Within several hours we were casting to rising brown trout on a small, clear river that bubbles across a moss-covered lava field, the massive ice field dominating the eastern horizon, now illuminated by red-gold 3:00 a.m. sunlight. There was not a tree in sight. It seemed mostly an illusion, accentuated by a healthy dose of New York-to-Iceland jet lag that surfaced shortly after we left the hotel parking lot.

Unreality is normal in my angling, as family and friends will readily verify, so when the opportunity to visit this strange, lovely land on the cheap arose, I took the bait and made plans to drag my confused act across the ocean. An editor at the *Denver Post* said she would run a story by me on the country and that was sufficient motivation for Icelandic Air (which owns the country, more or less) to provide free transportation. The airline runs like clockwork, serves great meals, and has an excellent maintenance record. The same efficiency cannot be ascribed to the national tourism ministry. Hotel rooms, rental cars, and related travel arrangements never materialized. One morning later in the trip the minister lied to our faces with a siding salesman smile concerning hotel arrangements in the small town of Hofn. There were no rooms waiting for us. We were literally stranded atop the fourth largest ice field in the world with no place to stay and no way down. As Tony said, dealing with the ministry "is like playing chess with a madman." Thankfully, despite the logistics problems, the Icelandic fishing proved highly pleasurable and rewarding.

Getting to the wild, only slightly-fished location was as much a part of the trip as the trout, the pristine country, and the camping. A paved highway that crossed

a number of rivers holding Atlantic salmon fresh from the sea led to a four-wheel drive track; then it was up along steadily narrowing gravel and dirt roads before fording a river that was headlight deep. The final push along inconspicuous tracks crossed sharp, crumbling lava beds that were a rugged reminder of the country's violent creation. Less than 10 inches of rain falls here per year, though over 160 inches pelts the interior of the nearby ice field. The mean annual temperature is just above freezing. The surface rock is anywhere from 700,000 years to more than 3 million years old. Volcanoes have erupted in the last thousand years minutes from our campsite. The country is treeless.

We raised tents and ate herring sandwiches before we rigged our rods and began fishing in the bright light of somewhere-past-midnight. Within minutes some of us caught browns and char on patterns ranging from Mickey Finns to caddis to that western U.S. standby, the Woolly Bugger. From day one the fishing was constant and good for browns to four pounds and char to twenty inches in this uninhabited region of northcentral Iceland called Arnarvatnsheioi (one of the easier names around here to pronounce). The choice of fly patterns was meaningless on these rivers, streams, and lakes that rarely, if ever, see the attentions of anglers. Everything we tried worked. The trout were plentiful, unsophisticated, and easy to catch. One of our guides, Gudmundar (Gummé) Jonsson, had never used a Woolly Bugger, but after this trip he mentioned that he might like to try fishing "just a little bit with that ugly fly." We gave Gummé a half dozen of them, secure in the knowledge that we'd left another purist lying in the volcanic dust.

The next day, June 21, was the longest day of the year. The sun was with us all of the time here just south of the Arctic Circle a half dozen hours north by northeast of Reykjavik. Under constant daylight, time becomes irrelevant and chasing fish is a twenty-four-hour proposition, limited only by the need for sleep.

Acerrano handed me a rum-and-coke and said it was cocktail time. I looked at my watch and indeed it was five—5:00 *a.m.* Time is relative. We reclined on foam pads and sleeping bags, exhausted in the best of ways, from working a fly line over new water. Our Icelandic guides, now turned fast friends, were busy making still more sandwiches of herring, some sort of smoked meat, and mysuostur (a brown cheese), all piled on top of split loaves of bread that went at least two feet. They said they were saving local delicacies like *svio* (singed sheep heads), *svioasulta* (sheep-head jelly and doesn't your mouth water pondering this toothsome delight), *hrutspungar* (ram testicles), and *skata* (fermented skate). I could hardly wait for dinner much later that day. I'm sure Tony felt the same.

"Well Holt, here's to being here, wherever that is," Tony toasted with a streetwise smile. "This sure doesn't look like Wrigley Field to me." We were both originally from the Chicago area and both Chicago sports addicts, a deadly affliction. No, we weren't at the ballpark and we weren't casting Elk Hair Caddis flies on Rock Creek. We were many lurching miles deep into the heart of this volcanic island, a place like none I'd ever seen.

This really was the middle of nowhere. The only other anglers we saw had also weathered the "roads" to these interior lakes. Their camp was somewhat more exotic than ours—including a large, bright-yellow tent emblazoned with the Smirnoff logo on all four sides. They partied constantly and I never did see any of them fish. These happy souls were our only "human" contact back here.

Breakfast the next day was an experience that included marinated herring, sausage, and surmjolk, a liquid form of yogurt and a dandy way to kick off the day. But not nearly so dandy as taking a bite of well-rotted shark fin. Rotted flesh reeking of ammonia and other flavors too awful to contemplate. Gummé said that his people love this food because of the incredible burst of flavor it provides. I can imagine.

Sharing experiences is part of travel to distant lands, or so I'm told. With that international spirit of communion in mind, we gave Gummé a maduro Honduran cigar of epic proportions. He inhaled a third of it, then tottered off across the moss before collapsing like a cheap tent struggling against a light breeze. I was reminded of Jethro of the "Beverly Hillbillies" in his big-time movie director mode puffing on a stogie until he turns green and staggers back to bed.

The only negatives in this unique country are the clouds of midges that buzz head high whenever the wind dies. Swat them and they bite back with the intensity of a hot match tip. Allow them to land and take off at their discretion and they leave flesh alone. We found bug nets and a cavalier attitude the best protection against this swarming nuisance, until a cool breeze knocked them back to the ground cover. We frequently forgot that we were wearing the protection, however, and the netting quickly was marked with burn holes from cigarettes and ill-timed expectoration.

The positives are many: The friendship of the guides. Grilled lamb for dinner (our new friends were only kidding about the other delights; the lamb served in Iceland is as good as any and we could not get enough of the meat on this trip). An evening drink sipped while taking in a landscape of moss and water and rock and ice is memorable. Nothing in America is like this place. Nothing at all.

Fishing the interior is an excellent alternative to the country's famous and extremely pricey Atlantic salmon action. A day's outing on a top river can cost as much as $2,700 plus food and lodging, and even a day on an average stretch runs $400, if you're lucky. Pay less and you run a good chance of working salmonless water.

Add in the fact that many of the best salmon beats are paralleled or crossed by highways and secondary roads in heavily managed, agrarian surroundings, and this "legendary" experience becomes some of the most overhyped and expensive fishing in the world.

All of which makes chasing trout and char extremely attractive for anglers looking for an offbeat and reasonably priced trip to a little-known corner of the world. Just remember, everything in Iceland is expensive. A hamburger and a beer might cost $20. Fishing the interior—including a guide, rental vehicle, permits, and food—costs around $250 a day, and, considering the quality of the fishing and the scenery, it is a bargain. Airfare runs around $600 round-trip from New York.

The country's uninhabited center is dominated by towering ice fields that run anywhere from 5 to 125 miles long and thousands of feet thick. Melting water from the ice feeds countless rivers and lakes that by any standards receive scant pressure from anglers, and in some cases hold browns of over ten pounds and char approaching double digits. The glacier that drives the system we fished is called Langjokull. Its stark whiteness is the dominant feature as it rolls off into the distance for many miles in a roughly north-south direction. The current rage among Icelanders and other Europeans is to try and traverse these fields in a convoy of four-wheel drives. The mind of man is amazing at times.

The only way to tour the region is with an Icelandic guide and with a couple of sturdy four-wheel-drive vehicles. Getting lost and mechanical breakdowns are not uncommon. A spare rig beats walking back to town, such as they are way out on these lava beds. Guides are not abundant but can be located at fly shops in Reykjavik. Almost everyone speaks English (although not as well as Hank Williams Jr.), so communication is not a problem. With a little effort and money, the logistics of an interior trout adventure are easily hammered out. Probably the most productive plan of attack is to spend three days in the country, return to Reykjavik to clean up and regroup before planning a more intensive campaign to the location just visited or to similar spots farther north or in the east or south. The experiences of the initial tour provide a mostly painless (remember the midges) training course for the more serious and enjoyable work of a determined trout fanatic.

In Arnarvatnsheioi all of the water looks like it should be full of browns and char. Most of it is. The stream flowing alongside what passes for a road—dusty tracks mixed with rocks and boulders that are scattered with natural abandon—vibrates with overtones of the Madison River with its miles and miles of riffles and swirling bankside pockets.

Just ahead, a huge sapphire pool whirled beneath a forty-foot waterfall. The first cast of a Gray Ghost in the froth at the base of the cascade turned up a small, silvery char. The day was an Icelandic rarity—no clouds and a sky as blue as the water. Gray mountain ridges and the ice field, always the ice field, towered above us. Bunches of wildflowers glowed in the gray-green moss. A slight breeze held off a few of the biting bugs while terns talked to each other as they bounced among the damp rocks.

The char were everywhere on almost every cast. Green Bombers. Muddler Minnows. Royal Coachmen. Buggers. Zonkers. It didn't matter in this pool. Silvery female char maybe a foot long and males to twenty inches, with a suggestion of pink on the bellies and flanks and emerald on their backs, took anything that moved across the current. There was no sign that anyone had been here before. We fished this bend in the river for quite a while before striking off for a group of lakes we had spotted just over a nearby swell in the lava field.

The lake turned out to be shallow like many others in the region. A small stream jumped down through a boulder stream course lined with a thick carpet of moss and emerald green heather. Small clumps of white and soft purple wildflowers glowed in the clear light. Air pollution is nonexistent in this part of the country. On sunny days the landscape is revealed in such clarity that distant objects appear to be only a mile or so away instead of thirty or more. Shadows are sharp, black. Rocks leap up at you in striking relief. The images piling one upon the other overwhelm the senses with an intensity found only in the roughest high country of the northern Rockies.

The lake yielded a number of browns that came willingly to a quickly stripped streamer. We never saw a concerted rise during our stay though our guides mentioned that this happens frequently later in the year. The stream feeding the lake is a series of small, deep pools, perfect water for trout, though not the sort of habitat I would associate with browns back in Montana. More like water for westslope cutthroat or maybe small brookies. Casts that work the fly swiftly across the pockets turn trout with regularity, some to fifteen inches. The browns are fat and well marked but without red spots. They no doubt spawn in late summer, the equivalent of the fall runs back home, and light up at that time.

Looking at a map of this region, one is struck by the amount of water there is to fish. Hundreds and hundreds of unnamed lakes and rivers and tiny streams filled with the browns and arctic char. Enough water to fish forever, although the experience becomes intense due to the short summers this far north. The days are long, however, perpetually in light in June and part of July. Gummé tells us of a river with many threads of ice-cold, milky turquoise water that is fed by the melting ice field. He says that this has been fished only rarely by more adventuresome members of his fly fishing club and that there are browns two-thirds of a meter long (twenty-six inches) and char over five pounds. Not large by Northwest Territory standards, but big by landlocked standards. He adds that much of the braided water has never been fished and there are reports of lakes like the one we are working now that are filled with even larger trout. This is the stuff of fly fishing dreams.

The fishing portion of our visit ended all too quickly and the disorganized hell arranged by the tourism ministry awaited us in Reykjavik. Even the following days of mayhem, reservations never made, connections unheard of, and guides of invisible stature cannot diminish the wonder of the country's interior. I, for one, will be back for a longer stay.

Recovering from Iceland and reintroducing myself to Lynda and the kids required more than a week, as did catching up on work, correspondence, bills, and jobs around the house. Early July means a quick dash down to Georgetown Lake and an annual soiree featuring fishing from float tubes, good food, and assorted madness. Talia, Miller, and a few others would be there for the fishing that often yielded brook trout and rainbow of several pounds or more. Georgetown Lake is nearly three thousand acres lying in a bowl at 6,350 feet surrounded by the Flint, Anaconda, and Sapphire mountains. Forested hills roll off to the horizon. The lake is relatively developed by Montana standards with resorts and summer homes. Speedboats present a hazard to floaters who stray too far from the shore, but all of these detractions are worth the bother because there are big trout here.

My first few experiences with the lake were not the type to create lasting memories or breed fondness. The first time I fished the water, the largest trout I caught nearly drowned from the weight of the streamer's hook. And I never thought of the lake as scenic years ago when I'd pass by on U.S. Alternate 10. Then, a few years back, an autumn outing filled with fat, feisty, and brilliantly colored brook trout set me straight. Georgetown is indeed quality trout water.

Leaving Whitefish at four-thirty in the morning allowed me to reach the lake by nine. The sun was an intense disk and the day would be a warm one. The boys were already out on the water bobbing happily in the slight chop about a quarter of a mile from the boat-launching site. I rigged up and paddled down the shoreline. The ever-present Biggs Special trailed in the water well behind me. My friends had already taken several decent fish, and I hoped that the bright day would not mean an early end to the action. I needn't have worried.

As MDFWP biologist Wayne Hadley said to me once, "Turn me loose on this water and I'll make the fishing so good you'd be afraid to throw a stick in the water for your dog." That's Georgetown when it's on.

A hundred yards or more from shore the water is deep. A thick carpet of aquatic weeds covers the bottom, providing shelter for the brook trout and ideal habitat for a variety of insects including damsels, mayflies, caddisflies, and midges. Using a ten-foot sink-tip line and fifteen-foot leader tapered to 5X (perhaps a bit light) and making long casts toward shore was the ticket. After the cast landed on the water, some slack was stripped off the reel to compensate for the distance lost as the line sank to the top of the weed bed. Once there, determined by counting and some experimentation, I usually took trout with a couple of quick, brief retrieves and then a pause, repeated until all but the sinking portion of the line was recovered. After fifteen minutes of trying to establish a routine, a brook trout hit—tugging, pulling, and running around like a rec league basketball team—everywhere at once. The fish played out quickly and came to the tube on its side, the cream-colored belly shining in the sunlight. Blues, greens, reds, oranges, pinks, and golds shone in the water, but not as riotous as the display would be a few months from now during autumn spawning. The brookie was sixteen inches, about average for me. Others have taken much larger fish here. The rest of the morning and early afternoon produced more trout in the same range. It was a good day.

By then Talia had chicken roasting over a fire and the evening was filled with conversation about fishing, various guide wars, hunting prospects, and sports—the usual stuff. The Bitterroot crew headed home after dark, running back over Skalkaho Pass, a short haul compared to the Whitefish run. I drove down to I-90, turned east and headed up to a campsite alongside a delightful little river filled with brown trout. The next morning, as soon as I'd eaten and gotten waders on, I began working Elk Hairs tight to the brushy, overgrown banks. Browns, flashing copper along the streambed, were clearly nymphing, but I wanted to take the fish on top. This stream is one of the best and two hours of casting produced a few dozen browns running from eight to eighteen inches. Along one narrow run below some rusting car bodies (classic Montana habitat improvement) I turned up five browns by working my way upstream casting into each little notch of tree limbs. The fish would leap and splash as soon as they felt the bite of the hook and I lost one when the tippet tangled, then snapped in a dense clump of leaves and branches. There were brown trout all over the stream—next to submerged logs, alongside rotting fence posts, behind rocks, under the banks, everywhere. By noon I'd had my fill and drove past Nevada Creek, the Blackfoot, and the Swan River on the way home.

Most of us would consider killing for the fishing of the past thirty hours. That's how things are supposed to be out here.

Lightning tore through the dense clouds far above us and the thunder shook the gray thrustings of rock. The air was dead calm at eleven thousand feet. The surfaces of the lakes in this granite basin were pressed flat. In this eerie atmosphere even the soft riseforms of the trout disappeared quickly, forced into the water by the vengeance of this late-July storm.

Hanging out above timberline for large chunks of time creates strange, unfamiliar sensations in a body. The continual flashes and palpable booms added to the disorientation. Up here far above the civilized valleys, we were not just observing the wild preamble to a severe weather system. We were right in the middle of it. Thunder pounded through our guts into the ground. Electrons flowed through us to the rock peaks and snow fields.

Flash. Crackle.

"Whoa! That was a big mother," we shouted in unison. Or did we?

Rock beneath us seemed to vibrate to its own beat and we were physically shoved along by the storm. There was music here ... but at the moment the tune was unfamiliar, frightening.

I tossed away my metal rod case and daypack and hunched down away from the energy cruising the airwaves. Static charges teased the hair on my arms and buzzed in my hands. Soft green sparks jumped in ripples from my friend's fingers, seeking a grounded connection with the rock at our feet. There was a buzz resonating from granite speakers.

This is close ... way too close. The rod cases were humming. Was it our swan song? I'd been in this area before, but never so high. The adrenalin rush created a certain clarity. The fear felt great. Perhaps I'd soon be dead, but at the moment I felt really alive.

The whole trip had started a thousand feet below around a smoky morning fire in cold, coffee-spiced air. Our plan was a modest one—to catch golden trout in the high mountain lakes. Ten miles back in on our horses, in the northern third of the Bridger Wilderness of the Wind River Mountains in Wyoming, there are hundreds of gem-quality lakes calling always softly with the satin-smooth sound of waves washing steadily onshore. The wilderness suggested peace, tranquility, and a safe but pristine environment. Wrong again.

Most of the best lakes here are unnamed, unknown, and unfished, thankfully. They are wild with plenty of water that rarely sees people or fly rods. Some years they are left completely alone. Just the mountains and the leaping fish. This is mystical country for those of us who love the arcane territory inhabited by rare salmonids.

I like goldens, maybe more than any other trout species. At least right now that's how I feel. Next month the "like" might shift to brown trout or more likely, considering the time of the year, bull trout. And these passions translate into spur-of-the-moment, grab-the-fly-rods, pack-the-camera, off-into-the-middle-of-no-where perambulations.

For me, locating wild trout in feral surroundings is a way of stepping back in time, back to when I was a child with absolutely no idea of what responsibility was and thought the wooded lot next door was a long way from home. Every day was easy and fun and full of excitement. Pain was skinned knees and worry involved the complex question of what was for lunch—peanut butter-and-jelly sandwiches or tuna fish? Life was not always smooth sailing then, but not nearly as hard as I find trying to be an adult is today. Fly fishing in these mountains is at least a temporary escape from mortgages, insurance premiums, and earning a living. Casting to trout is much more than fun. It is a way to stay happy and to keep all of the day-to-day confusion in perspective.

The first few days of our outing were filled with nice trout in shocking colors—Technicolor escapees gliding away in a snowmelt creek that rushes into this emerald gem over a mile above the pedestrian life in the populated valley below. When we first crossed this stream on horseback, the clacking of the horses' hooves on the rocks sent dozens of the trout scurrying upstream in a mad flight to safety. The water was so shallow in places I could see the dorsal fins and dark backs of the fish stick out of water as they wriggled and splashed from us. Trout were everywhere in the stream. We had timed the trip perfectly. A week sooner and most of the fish would be holding down below in the deepwater recesses of the lake. A week later and the fish would be done spawning—exhausted, emaciated, and without spirit or fight. To find the goldens in the stream at this time in such fine condition was the rarest of good fortune. Almost as rare as the goldens themselves. Even fly fishers deserve favor on occasion.

Goldens were approaching spawning velocity so the four of us planned our angling and photographic approaches while sitting in the chill night around a wild blaze. Details were not left to chance. The vibrating urgency of a large trout at the end of a line is intoxicating stuff, but we would not play these fish to exhaustion. Just a taste of the action was all we wanted. Then the goldens would be released unharmed.

The two-hour trek to the golden water looked like a miniature assault on a Himalayan peak. Tripods. Fly rods. Lenses. Waders. Landing nets. Camera bodies. The trappings of an out-of-control obsession. Gear was unloaded. F-stops and depth-of-fields calculated. Rods

rigged and weighted. Muddler Minnows cast to the head of a small pool filled with bright fish.

The spawning ritual had produced a fantastic display of color in the goldens—metallic orange males and blood-red females. Groups of the females clustered around the largest and most brightly colored males. Size and color intensity determine dominance in trout. The best of the breed continue the lot. By any standard a two-pound golden is a big trout. Some of the males in this little stream weighed four, maybe five, pounds. Huge fish. The trout moved and swayed as one animal in the pool in a steady rhythm dictated by the stream's current. Special trout handled with care, to be quickly exposed to film and gently returned to the stream.

The first trout fought hard. I chased an orange-and-pink male weighing several pounds down and out of a sapphire pool through water that did not cover its back, over a small falls, and into two more pools. Sailing over the last drop-off, the golden crashed sideways into the water. Spray from the concussion arced up and away in a diamond circle. Tiring, the fish still struggled, using its body's resistance in the current as an ally against the constant pressure of the fly rod. The contest, flaring briefly to life when the trout pounced on the streamer, ended suddenly. The fish abruptly quit the game. While disengaging the hook, I admired this wonderful creature. In the crystal sunlight the fish radiated rare gold, orange, pink, green, and perfect white. After being gently revived in the easy flow near shore, the golden vanished somewhere in the sparkling water. I had held the fish in my hands, thrust above my head up into the sky—a silent, glowing offering to my special angling deity.

The four of us fishing together, laughing as the true children we were, enjoyed several hours of lunatic energy. This was trout magic in high-country, Wyoming style. Just the fish, the primitive, treeless mountains, and a couple of crazies safe at home in the middle of nowhere.

For two days straight our luck held. Angling gods take occasional pity on the derelict trout fanatics. This was our time and we jumped in way over our heads. Fishing. Photographing. Watching.

In the afternoon warmth, clad in chest-high neoprene waders, I stalked the shallow runs and riffles on my hands and knees, a waterproof camera looped around my neck. The goldens were intent upon the spawning dance and with patience and a modest degree of stealth I was able to creep to within a few feet of the trout as they held in small pools before me. I dunked the camera in the ice-cold stream and aimed as best I could. The flash had no effect on the fish. They just continued to move from side to side in the current, holding position in the pack. I exposed three rolls of film in hopes of getting one decent shot.

"Holt, you look like you're ready for the rubber room the way you're all hunched over there," I heard from a voice on the bank. A friend, towering above me, grinned around a pipe stem, blue smoke curling in the air. " World famous bozo loses it at eleven thousand feet. " I see it all now. I figured you had at least a couple of years to go before you snapped."

"Snapped, hell! I'm getting some great shots here."

"You're just looking for a free ride on the Thorazine express. I know your scams."

Mountain craziness is a much sought after disease that once contracted is never fully shaken. The grip of this mental virus is tenacious, never going fully dormant even in the dark depths of winter.

Next morning after breakfast, my friend and I decided we'd make a day hike to examine smaller waters that we'd glimpsed previously from our horses. The others were going to fish a lake just below camp during our absence. Off the two of us went, sumptuously provisioned with beef jerky, a few bottles of beer, and cheap cigars. First class all the way.

A huge boulder field tumbled down from the lakes above. Jagged peaks cornered the western horizon. Travel was difficult here. There was the stream cascading down to the trout-filled lake below us. The goldens here were smaller but still present in force. Perhaps bigger specimens swam the isolated riffles and pools farther on—holdovers from other breeding runs. We were greedy and wanted to know. Rod cases make adequate walking sticks anyway. The climb was steep and the way confusing and there were not many trout in this thread of water. A few small, dark green pools punctuated with spooky fish dashed away from the vibration of our footfalls. The stream was bordered by wildflowers splashed with sunlight—waves of white columbine, Indian paintbrush, and others I could not name.

We located good numbers of golden fry but no trout of substance and no spawning beds in the brightly colored gravel. How the small fish arrived in these crystal-clear, moonshine flows was a mystery. These places hidden in the narrow, twisting miniature canyons of shattered rock appeared to be ideal brood areas, which perhaps they were at other times.

We smoked cigars in a gap between a huge mantel of tilted igneous rock marked with striations of black, slate, and rust. The cut led to a dry fall that tumbled down hundreds of feet to a game trail winding through pond-nourished grasses and moss below. The other day we'd seen a cow moose and her calf moving silently along here in the dawn mists.

"Jesus. These things are awful. I thought nickel cigars were a dead issue."

"Yeah. I figured you'd like 'em. Taste great up here with this expensive beer, don't they?"

"Buck-a-six-pack beer. Where do you find this stuff?"

Clouds of acrid smoke hung discretely in the still, heavy air. Mosquitoes made brief suicide runs into the blue haze, only to retreat in looping, dazed flight to fresh air.

"Look at that one bugger. I think the smoke killed him."

"Mosquito hell awaits me. Who sold you these things anyway?"

"There are fifty more at camp."

"That's nice."

A tiny lake tucked well back in an isolated nook of this plateau was our next stop. We struck out as obvious storm warnings vibrated on the craggy northern horizon. We were determined when it came to finding goldens and continued the hike despite the approaching weather.

And that's how we had gotten to where we are. Hunched down together trying to light more cheap cigars as the wind, rain, and hail came at us. Puffing away intently as though we were condemned men offered a ritual last smoke. Nowhere to run. Nowhere to hide. Things were so vivid I could feel the hum of the whole world, could taste in the harsh tobacco smoke the character of the Honduran soil where the leaves of my cigar had grown. I could sense everything, like a claustrophobic approaching a dark cave. We were joined with the forces of nature here in the afternoon darkness. The clouds moved right through us. Lightning crashed into rocks. The thunder was deafening. And the wind wailed through the fissures. Talk was impossible with wildness rushing everywhere.

Amazingly the moose and her offspring again loped past us, not fifty yards away in the surreal dimness of the angry weather. The animals seemed to move with, to be a part of, the storm. Soon they vanished in a spinning mass of dark clouds beyond the near ridgeline.

"Boom!"

Except for the loud ringing in my ears, I could not hear anymore, but I could still see as my rod case, now riddled with holes by a lightning bolt like a beer can blasted by a twelve-gauge turkey load, went careening over a pile of rock, pieces of smoking graphite fly rod waving from the jagged wounds. What was left of my daypack was smoldering in a small crater. No words were needed. We both took off running as fast as we could, jumping the gaps between the boulders as we frantically worked our way down to camp. Instinctively we hit the ground whenever the lightning and thunder went off around us.

Things were ugly and I was scared to death and certain I was going to die. The storm lasted forever and was over in an instant. The sensation of being wet and cold returned and was welcome. We looked at each other and laughed, but not like yesterday or the day before it—

that was a laugh of joy brought on by the fish. This was more like surviving a high-speed crash on the Interstate.

The blues and grays of our tents were visible on the knoll above a little lake that was dotted with riseforms of feeding goldens. The location looked safe and comfortable. Sort of like home. We were shot and evening was coming on. A warm fire and some hot food would be damn good.

Later that night after dinner, while sipping some Irish coffee, the sky cleared revealing a jet-black loneliness dotted with stars. The wind was now dead and the storm well past when a swift and familiar insight struck, painlessly: Often the best times on a trip dedicated to fishing do not include trout. But hell, I knew that. The fish were just an excuse to hang out in the open and wait for whatever came my way.

The trip into the Wind Rivers was ideal, without flaw, but it was now time to focus on the fishing in my part of the world. Early August means chasing bull trout with large streamers. This is also the time when the many mountain lakes and dashing, wild-hearted streams are at their best. And there are the underrated fly fishing lakes in Glacier Park and some fine action down on the Flathead Indian Reservation just over an hour from my front door. This is no time to be on the road in search of angling adventure. First up will be some serious casting for native bull trout.

People are strange when you're a stranger.
Faces look ugly when you're alone.

This was not good. When lyrics to an old Doors ditty bounce along the labyrinthine pathways of my brain and start to sound profound, can the breakup of reality be far behind? Music like this is always wandering through my mind while fishing.

It is mesmerizing to stand hip deep in a small northwestern Montana river and throw weighted Woolhead Bendbacks far upstream (patterns better suited to saltwater fishing), swiftly mend line, and follow the drift on its way down. To lose concentration for even a second can mean losing the one chance of the day to connect with a huge trout, although it is almost an axiom in my angling that the minute my mind drifts, the fish show up.

This casting is tough. You dig a quarter-mile of sink-tip line out of the water, fling it upstream with a midcourse correction that ricochets off the top of your head, then back cast while ducking as the fly whistles past the ears (either one, it does not matter) before a quick haul sends the red-and-white melange skipping across the river's surface to the top of a short, gravel cutbank run.

Hey! Chasing the elusive bull trout can approach the rare status of just "too much fun," perhaps not quite as much fun as dodging lightning bolts in the Wind Rivers, but a good time nonetheless. My arm and shoulder hurt from the repetitive casting and my brain was baked from the sun. And this was nowhere near the end of this delightful fiasco.

Everyone knows what bull trout are, right?

Bull trout used to be called Dolly Varden until fisheries biologists determined that the two were different creatures, at least morphologically speaking. Dollies are still *Salvelinus malma*, but bulls are now *Salvelinus confluentus*. The differences don't stop with names. All trout, once they hit a certain size, like to eat other fish, but to examine the head and jaws of a big bull is to see the results of a wild, free-swinging ride through evolution. Bull trout are the sharks of the freshwater salmonid clan. Compared to Dolly Varden, their skulls are flattened and widened to facilitate eating small whitefish, squawfish, ciscos, sculpins, and other trout, along with the occasional slowly rusting chrome bumper from an abandoned Studebaker. They grow to over twenty pounds and in the Flathead River system they average over eight. We're not talking Smoky Mountain brook trout here, though they are related and the species also has a good deal of genetics in common with lake trout and arctic char.

All the same, the bull trout is a freshwater animal that thrives in pristine lakes and rivers, country that has not been scalped by logging or leveled by developers. Needless to say, but worth mentioning, there are not a lot of these fish around.

Not many people know very much about bull trout, except, that is, for the boys down at the Region I office of the MDFWP. Some of these fisheries biologists can tell a person where the fish will be to within a few feet and a few days when the bulls are running in the rivers as they obey their annual procreational imperative.

"I want one of those. No, make that *need* one of those," I said, pointing a crooked finger at a photograph of a bull lit up like a brook trout Christmas tree.

"Yeah. I bet you do," said one of the fishery guys as he turned around in his chair to admire the print tacked to his office wall—a photograph showing a fish that had last seen five pounds several holiday seasons ago. "Your hands always shake like that? I really would like to take you out on the river and show you some myself, but I'm buried in survey work, so I can't, but I'll tell you where to find them," he added.

Actually I think he was more than a touch leery of spending time with someone he considered a bit unstable. But he did direct me to the bulls and that's where I was at the beginning and we'll head back there later.

My fascination with bull trout began in earnest late one winter when a "bull trout expedition" began to surface among a couple of friends who were intrigued by the obscure nature of the species. Oh sure, I'd taken the fish many years ago in the Bob Marshall Wilderness casting those famous red-and-white spoons far out into a deep isolated lake. And I'd even caught a few small ones on streamers in the North Fork of the Flathead River running along the western edge of Glacier National Park, but never a bull of size, color, and distinction.

Planned for late June, the trip was a roaring failure, doomed by a warm and occasionally blue Montana sky. Heavy snows the previous winter and a late runoff sealed our fate. We chased bulls futilely in the raging, discolored waters of both the North Fork of the Flathead and Swan rivers, never turning the much-sought-after species. One of our party, in a heroic effort, pulled a cutthroat from the North Fork on a streamer. The fish appeared so stunned that anyone would even consider working the river during these conditions that it swam meekly to net.

We fished likely looking points that we'd spotted while cruising the highway above Swan Lake. Pulling over to the side of the road, we'd scramble down steep earthen banks and cast large streamers futilely for hours. Cast and retrieve. Cast and retrieve. All with the same results. Nothing. Absolutely nothing. And we hiked through prime grizzly country along the Canadian border in search of bulls in a timber-shrouded, deep-dark lake only to be greeted with the sight of several of our northern, nonbear brethren trolling up and down the middle of the pond, killing cutthroat trout, motors belching blue smoke that hung lifelessly along the surface of the water. The "foreign" side had a boat launch accessible by road. We searched the water along our shoreline diligently using an assortment of gaudy patterns to no avail. Again, absolutely nothing.

In our desperation we raced across Glacier Park, up and over the Going-to-the-Sun Road to the distant flatlands that hold the fecund lakes of the Blackfeet Reservation east of the Continental Divide. We knew the bull trout were now a bad dream and we wanted to catch a trout, to feel the throb of a strong fish at the ends of our lines. And the Reservation cooperated with big rainbows. But that's another story for another time.

So the June bull trout extravaganza was something of a failure. One friend flew back home to New York a broken man. Another is no longer working at his job for the state in Helena. He was banished to the far Pacific

Rim, dutifully manning his agency's office in Kumamoto City, Japan.

Bull trout are like that. They can disrupt lives and destroy fantasy, but then if you have ever fished hard for big trout, you know what I am saying.

Tom Weaver, another MDFWP fisheries biologist, called one morning and said he and a crew would be electroshocking a stretch of creek up the North Fork, making a count of small bull trout to see how the fish were doing. There was a chance of turning a big fish, he added, just in case I still wanted to see one. And, of course, I did. Fly fishing for me is much more than merely catching rainbows, browns, and brookies in waters where I have always caught them in the past. Part of the romance of the pursuit is tracking down little-known populations of rare species in out-of-the-way parts of the world. The mystery and excitement of the chase are important aspects of the game—both in my fishing and my pedestrian life. Wondering what past-due bills will come in the day's mail is a time-honored variation of this theme.

An hour-and-a-half later I was walking slowly down a gravel bank with Weaver while his crew rigged a catch net at the bottom of the run they were to work and dragged a gas-fired generator upstream to power the electrodes that would stun the fish. The biologist walked out on a downed log and peered beneath looking for fish that might be hiding from daylight. None were there, but he pointed out a large redd or spawning site the fish had dug recently.

"They're moving gravel at night," said Weaver, demonstrating the bull's activity with his hands, palms together, making a flapping motion. "They can move some big rock, especially the larger fish."

You had to agree. This redd was over six inches deep, six or seven feet square. Plenty of the displaced rocks were several inches in diameter. When it came to breeding, these trout took their work to heart.

"This is prime water, but we've had trouble up here. Someone, and I know who he is, drove his truck right up the streambed herding the fish into a net at night. Then the bastard had the nerve to drag a gunny sack of them into a bar and brag about it," said Weaver, who did not look happy now. "I had men camp out on that logging road up there for a week and we never did catch him, but we will."

Weaver went silent and stared up at the logging road and then back down at the stream next to him. He muttered something I could not understand, then walked away from the water.

We worked downstream. Weaver dug into the gravel to kick up tiny bull trout that bury themselves for safety. Moving from side to side, he cast the metal electrode as the gas generator buzzed away on the shore. The electrode was attached to what looked like the end of a hefty rake handle and he flung it all over the stream course, its clanging echoing back and forth in the valley. He worked the water thoroughly.

Fish from an inch to maybe six inches floated up and were quickly captured by the nets. They were dumped into buckets to be counted and measured later. There were dozens of trout swimming in the pails and only one bull trout looked dead. The benefits of the data gained here far outweigh the loss of a few trout, though even the few mortalities bother Weaver, and I understand his feelings. The loss of any wild thing is sad and frustrating, especially when you are working like hell to save it from extinction. The only way to preserve these dwindling populations of unique fish is to learn everything there is to know about them. How many are left? What streams do they live in? What times of the day do they migrate, feed, and breed? How large do they get? But all of this attention sometimes results in inadvertent deaths. Weaver, along with the rest of us who love trout, pull for the fish to make successful spawning runs, to survive and even flourish despite the heavy odds stacked against them. The threats are considerable—poachers, raging floods, logging, road building, and death from predators like eagles and martens and man. Bull trout live a tough life from day one.

"The big fish, which really take a charge, are rarely harmed," he said as the electrode clanged off some barely submerged rocks.

Then, next to us there was a "whoosh," a big-fish sound and a large swirl, but no one saw a fish. As the biologists worked closer to the net a huge bull suddenly thrashed in the current and tried to blast its way to freedom upstream. Swiftly moving rubber boots splashed back and forth across the gravel and boulder streambed as Weaver guided the excited trout into a net with judicious use of the electricity. One last jolt forced the fish into a large net that one of the biologists had trouble lifting, even with both hands. The metal pole attached to the sack sagged under the weight of the bull trout.

"Holy shit!" was all I could say; doesn't it always seem that poetry is spontaneous at times of high excitement.

The bull that Weaver hefted was impressive and we all admired the fish. Olive green back and flanks studded with orange spots and a big bronze-gold belly. A trophy fish.

"A male waiting in case any more females run up here to spawn. I'd guess between thirteen and fourteen pounds. Nice fish. Boy, did your eyes bug out, John."

We laughed because we knew this fish was unique. Hell, they all are. This one was running up out of

a vicious torrent filled with rocks and that explode as they are propelled into each other by the mad water, downed trees swirling in eddies like match sticks, and local "sportsters" trying to snag them from the river with treble hooks and doorknobs for sinkers. This trout had come nearly one hundred miles from the lake, past small cities, beneath concrete highway bridges that gave way to small wooden structures crossing cold-water streams dashing over colorful gravels.

"A lot of them make it (spawning) once, fewer do it twice," said Weaver as he released the trout, which, though still addled, moved to the far side of the stream, wanting no part of us, its back and dorsal fin exposed to the air in the too-shallow water. "Not many ever get back three times. They live a hard life."

They sure do and in some of the best country anywhere. Mountains are everywhere—timber covered (although, unfortunately, clear-cut in places) and snow covered. Grizzlies, elk, eagles, wolves, and occasionally mountain caribou hang out here, but I think these bull trout in their own low-key way make a pretty convincing statement about the wild.

So we're back to the beginning and the day is hot and clear. One of those late-summer magic days that Montana prides itself on. The stretch of river is right where the biologist said it would be. It is the one I reached only after walking through the trees, wading across a road submerged by a beaver dam, hiking across a mud flat covered with mountain lion tracks, and, finally, crossing a wide, mounded gravel bar.

Yes, this is the place in spades. While I rig up, two bull trout break the surface for reasons I can only guess at. Their spawning pink stomachs flash in the light. The swirls from the rises are right along the bank just a few feet below the small grassy point, exactly where the biologist said I'd find fish. I am impressed. The forested mountains dance emerald green in the sky and a little creek curls into the river. The bulls wait patiently for slightly cooler water to trigger their drive up this dandy liquid piece of work that is their home stream. Although it is not twenty feet wide, the fish will run a couple of miles upstream, moving through deep pools and splashing across bubbling riffles to the clean, time-honored gravels to spawn in secret, away from my probing attentions.

And that is as things should be.

I've been skillfully casting this rig for hours now and the back of my head hurts like someone whacked it with a baseball bat. Saltwater patterns like Woolhead Bendbacks are damn heavy. Strip in a foot of line. Mend some slack upstream to extend the drift of the fly. Strip. Mend. Full-stop.

Full-stop? What? Bottom? A log?

Raising up on the rod brings with it the roll of a huge fish and I catch a quick sight of it spinning hot pink and dark green on the surface before it turns and runs slowly downstream. This bull is not going to stop. The reel's drag buzzes mechanically as the trout moves toward a gray logjam, fast water, and freedom a quarter-mile away. I follow sinking and slipping in the small, smooth gravels and shallow water. I put some pressure on the fish, knowing that while the 3X tippet is strong enough under normal trout fishing conditions, it is not nearly hefty enough for working a large bull. I'm so nervous and excited I have trouble breathing normally. After what seems like a long time we are just above the jam. The bull trout is some eight feet away, and it looks like a slightly smaller version of the one Weaver found. Much too deep in the body to be covered by the water near shore. I slowly pull him to me.

"Please God. Come on man. Give a derelict a break."

"Come on," I say, muttering the prayer always offered when we really want a fish. "Come on."

"Damnit!"

The tippet snaps. The connection is over and the fish knows it, moving slowly, almost arrogantly away from me and then sinking into the deep run on the far bank, where it disappears from sight. Only the sounds of water sliding downstream and the demented clackings of airborne grasshoppers remain.

Somehow despair inspires in me a perfect blend of strength, motion, and coordination as I pivot around, away from the river, back and shoulders tightly flexed, and launch rod and reel, grip-first, toward a stand of tall pines behind me. Light sparkles from the graphite and I imagine the sound of the rod whistling through the air as it describes a perfect, black arc before disappearing from view.

The fish is gone. The rod is gone. I am gone. This bull trouting is strange, powerful stuff.

Next year, buddy ... next year ...

But there was to be no next year. The number of bull trout redds, a means of determining population figures, reached disastrously low levels. The MDFWP, in its infinite wisdom, closed the season on bull trout for every water west of the Continental Divide, except for two lakes. This makes tremendous sense: Penalize the hell out of fly fishers and others while the Forest Service and private timber companies work concertedly, in violation of many federal and state regulations, to clear-cut the forests of Montana. Precluding fly fishers from chasing bull trout eliminates a potentially powerful and wealthy segment of the public from the fight to save the species. How can someone from Boston take up the cause if he never has an opportunity to experience the power and magic of the fish wailing away at the end of his line? Add the predacious behavior of lake trout (the ones I've caught and killed for the table have been stuffed with juvenile bull trout), the loss of habitat from development, and assorted other threats, and even a blind man can see why the fish are in trouble.

Closing the season reeks of politics, bureaucratic nonsense, expediency, and a childish fear of criticism. Far better to anger fly fishers than the timber industry or the rapacious horde of developers and realtors that has invaded the state like a pack of vermin. Those groups have money and clout. Never mind doing what is right and taking a public stand against the rape of the woods and fields. That has the potential to rock the boat, to stir controversy. The state has decided instead to brainwash the angling populace, which is easier to manipulate.

I hope the char survive, but attempting to stop fishing for the bulls is futile. And there will always be poaching. Enforcement has never been effective in this area. There are too few wardens and far too much land to cover.

So that we all understand each other here, let me say that I am going to fish for bull trout in direct contravention of this asinine change in regulations. Call the decision civil disobedience. Call it contrariness. Call it whatever you wish. I'm still going to fish for bull trout in late July and early August with barbless hooks. Just one or two fish. I need to know if any are still out there.

Some of the finest and most interesting fishing in Montana is located on the seven Indian Reservations, most notably the Blackfeet, Crow, Northern Cheyenne, and Flathead. The three others, Fort Peck, Fort Belknap, and Rocky Boys also offer fishing but they are located well out on the northern high plains in isolated, arid country. The action on the Reservations is tough to find. You need to know where you are going in this country.

The Flathead is only an hour from Whitefish and provides a bit of everything. There is rugged, high mountain lake and stream fishing in some of the most spectacular land found anywhere, provided you are in excellent shape to hike in, which means straight up much of the way. There is bass fishing in several large reservoirs and there are spring creeks and rivers down on the valley floor holding fair numbers of westslope cutthroat, brook, rainbow, and brown trout. There are also bull trout, but they have been off limits for years, even to tribal members. There is also a large amount of primitive land set aside for the tribe, a place for them to practice ancient beliefs and rituals undisturbed. These areas are clearly marked and should be honored.

The moving water found in the valley attracts my attention. It is enjoyable to drive down past Flathead Lake in the late afternoon heat. The Mission Mountains seen through the haze seem to waver on the east side of the lake. Low hills and rock abutments drift off to the west, their flanks covered with grasses and brush turned the color of buckskin by the summer sun. A small river flows out of the Missions and joins up with the Clark Fork River after a twenty-mile journey through farmland and wide-open range. Buffalo, deer, grizzlies, and rattle-snakes can be spotted along the drainage at times. The stream is perhaps thirty- to fifty-feet wide with tree-lined or brushy undercut banks. Riffles pour into lazy pools and slick glides. Midstream rocks provide plenty of pock-ets to pick. This is ideal holding water for browns to fifteen inches, maybe a touch larger on a propitious out-ing, often in autumn. There are loads of mountain white-fish here, too.

During the dog days of summer, casting dries during the middle of the afternoon is futile. Nymphs are the only answer. But nymphing frequently becomes an exercise in exasperation with the whitefish checking in at a four (or higher) to one ratio with the browns. That is the reason for the late start. Caddis dependably come off the water right before dusk. A tan #14 Elk Hair worked along the edges of current seams or tight against the bank will take plenty of browns, stacked up in the prime runs to take advantage of the evening banquet. You can spot trout snouts bobbing up and down in the diminish-ing light. The stream is simple to wade, easy to read, and a joy to fish. An old pair of Converse high-tops with felt glued to the soles, a pair of jeans, a shirt with deep pockets, a small box of bugs, tippet material, floatant, and a pocket knife—that's all there is to it.

I park my truck beneath a clump of aspens. The two-weight is rigged and the sun is glowing orange near the horizon. Several browns are working steadily along the bank below. They are afraid of nothing at the moment. The noise from their sippings sounds like someone abruptly closing open hands on the surface of still water. A small game-fishing trail leads downstream, offering an easy and undetected approach to the fish. The water feels cool, almost soft, pushing gently against my legs. I wade quietly and make a short cast to the outer edge of the current, the one farthest from the bank, that drops the fly with a slight curve in the leader at the lower end of the run. The caddis bobs downstream for no more than three feet before a trout takes. The fish stirs the current and I force it quickly down out of the holding water, away from the other browns. It comes quickly to my hand. Perhaps twelve inches of perfection, this brown has classic markings with enough blood-red spotting to set off the more subdued shades of bronze, yellow, brown, black, and off-white.

Browns may not be in the electric, neon, eye-popping class of spawning brookies and goldens, but they are the trout of choice for me right at this moment. They are secretive, predacious, and ideally formed to attack forage fish and skittering insects on and in the water. Browns are strong, aggressive and they can be maddeningly difficult to catch. They are an honest fish, though. If a fly fisher reads the water, the conditions, and the hatches right and then makes a solid presentation, he will take a few of them. This is unlike working over cruising and rising goldens that will examine every feathered piece of barbed foolishness in your fly boxes with excruciating slowness and apparent disdain before drifting casually over to dine on a natural that looks identical to your fly. Other trout species display a capricious nature at times, browns being browns will hit an appropriate food source whenever it is presented properly. That's the trick, but at least a legitimate one.

Three more browns, one of sixteen inches, fall to the Elk Hair in the run. Working the riffle above this produces two others. A beaver dam has created a waterfall and below it a large, foaming pool. The water shines like quicksilver, thick and heavy. Larger fish are feeding, creating clusters of concentric rings on the still surface at the tail and along the calm flanks of the hole. The fish will be wary here. If I take more than two I will be pleased. Working from right to left seems to be the way.

A slight curve cast next to the bubbles and a brief float takes number one. The brown pressures the light rod as it tries to reach the root-choked undercut bank, but fails. I hold it briefly and then slip the hook from the corner of its jaw. Another cast toward the center of the water takes number two—a leaping, thrashing crasher that is better fish, perhaps seventeen inches. But its commotion puts down all but three trout lined up on the far left side of the pool. Not wading, but pivoting slightly at the waist, I make a cast of thirty feet, long for this water, to the lower end of the glide and a brown snaps at the fly and is on, running in tight circles below the surface before playing out. This is great. I feel like I know what I'm doing. Three trout. Perhaps one more with a touch of luck. But I am too eager and I rush the next cast. The fly plunks down hard in front of the second brown which stops rising. The last trout is still working a few yards farther up. I lay down the final offering in a bubbling chute directly above the trout which has no choice but to take the imitation. No longer worried about spooking the pool, the trout has carte blanche to vent its frustration at my cruel ruse. It makes several sharp runs, a leap, and some surface disturbance before the struggle ends. Nine fish in less than an hour. More than enough. I walk back to the truck, change to dry socks and moccasins, crack a cold beverage, and take in the evening while sitting on the tailgate. Smoke from a Jamaican cigar rises slowly.

Crickets are chirping in almost perfect counterpoint to the unpredictable rhythm of the flowing water. Bats are silhouetted against a deep purple sky full of bright stars and planets. A faint breeze rustles the leaves and cools my face. There are no other cars, no lights, no other sounds. Maybe I'll remain here until dawn.

Every one of my friends and family who live outside of Montana has an obsession with bears, mainly grizzlies. When I tell them of some outrageous country filled with special fishing and complete solitude, land that is tucked far back beneath some glacial cirque, they always ask, "What about the bears? What about all of those bears, John?"

Well what about the bears? I'm glad they're around. My chances of dying at the claws of an enraged grizzly are far less than they were when I used to back-stop my friend John Glisch as he covered the SWAT team trying to pop some drug-crazed murderer in Beloit, Wisconsin, back in both of our early newspaper days. When I'm in the out-of-touch country way back from anywhere I watch myself. I make enough noise to let everyone, especially my good buddies the grizzlies, know I'm in the neighborhood. It would be hideous, both for myself and the bear, to have surprised one and ended up getting mauled.

So, what about the bears? The following account contains far less hyperbole than stodgy government officials and others would like to believe. Most of this, you decide what is real and what is not, took place in country visible from the upper deck of my home. May it always be so.

"There goes another one," screamed my companion with a cracking, high-pitched voice.

But she was right—it was another grizzly, this time a five- or six-hundred pound boar. The bears were everywhere. Since we'd started up a trail toward Upper Kintla Lake in Glacier National Park, grizzlies had appeared constantly, downhill to the right of us, loping past us in twos, threes, and fours, or meandering through the pines. Not one of them acted like it had gotten wind of us, or if it had, there were apparently bigger doings in the woods this day.

Running into a grizzly in the back country of Glacier goes with the territory. It is part of the "charm" of hiking in the park. Every season some hapless visitor from Peoria, Illinois, is chased up a tree by a bear, then usually hauled back down and chewed on to the tune of a hundred or so stitches. Deaths are rare—only a half dozen or so in the park's history—and the end result is usually a photo of the victim in a hospital bed and a lengthy interview in one of the local papers about how a crazed 35,000-pound deranged animal with glowing red eyes savagely attacked the innocent bystander without provocation. Sometimes the injured party sues the Park Service, hoping to make a quick killing (having only recently avoided a similar fate at the paws of the bears). A media-type attorney handles the case, which draws a

good deal of attention from the press, but life goes on for the bears and the park in general.

So what was happening with the bears? Nothing was out of the ordinary. The sky was a perfect, deep blue. The temperature was in the low eighties with a light breeze lending a soft counterpoint to the peculiar situation. The two of us had already seen over thirty of the legendary creatures—more than we'd sighted, total, in our lives. Stranger yet, the bears ignored our presence. Even sows with cubs, usually a deadly combination, were unconcerned. True, the park has been overrun with hikers, neophyte nature freaks, health fanatics, and assorted other crazies. And, yes, the bears have lost some of their fear of humans, but what was taking place in this part of the woods today was not normal.

"I don't get it. We should be dead by now. I've never been that close to a bear before."

"There go two more," said Anne with a glazed expression.

Just up the trail a couple of medium-sized males ambled across the trail and down to Kintla Creek, flowing with benign indifference not far below us in the dense lodgepole pine.

"I'd say let's get the hell out of here, but I don't know where that is. Bears to the right of us. Bears to the left of us. Stuck in the middle again."

"Cut the comedy. Do we go up or down?" she insisted.

Desperate times call for desperate measures. I cracked open the bottle of bourbon I'd carefully stashed in my pack and took a healthy swallow before passing it over to my tightly wound friend. It was a 1.75 liter jug, but this was intended to be a four-day trip and the potential for things turning ugly was ever-present. Eight ounces of whiskey per person per day was cutting it a bit thin, but both of us had known adversity before. No bears sighted in the last ten minutes, maybe their bizarre behavior was over. No one would believe what had happened today, whatever "that" was.

Grizzlies are known for their unpredictable behavior. They had killed two nineteen-year-old women on the same night in August 1967 in different parts of Glacier—only the second and third bear-related fatalities at the time. The bears would also gather on Huckleberry Mountain in pursuit of the hill's bountiful namesake, and some animals would converge on McDonald Peak in the Mission Mountains just south of here to feed on army cutworm moths of all things. It was a social event, like fly fishers gathering on the Madison for the salmonfly hatch.

A park ranger who knew this area as well as anyone had been dragged down by a female grizzly in a surprise attack a couple of years back, too. He had been looking for an airman on leave from Malstrom Air Force Base in Great Falls. The man was thought to be either drowned in Bowman Lake or making a damned good effort to have things look that way. The bear came out of the brush with swift and sure vengeance, smashing the ranger down with a vicious swipe at the man's leg. After what must have seemed like an extended trip to hell, the bear was driven off by, of all things, a punch to the nose. Fending off an enraged grizzly with a pop to the chops seems as likely as stopping a logging truck with a snowball, but who can argue with success. The ranger escaped with a badly mangled leg and his life. The bear vanished back into the mountains. The missing airman's body was eventually found tangled in a logjam at the outlet of the lake. "Permanently absent without leave" the boys in nearby Martin City liked to say over lukewarm beers and shots of whiskey.

> *Oh when I'm dead an' in my grave,*
> *An' no more whiskey will I crave,*
> *On my tombstone let this be wrote,*
> *'Ten thousand quarts run down his throat!'*

Anne took another pull from the liquor and passed it back to me while a huge cinnamon-colored bear, smelling for all the world like a high school locker room, padded by. The big guy stopped, looked us both over, and let out a soft, cynical "woof." More whiskey. Anne just shook her head. This trip was beyond her control and she laughed before nodding off into warm afternoon sun.

Glacier was magic country. Members of the Blackfeet tribe had always stayed away from its rugged interior. Perhaps because of the few who did stumble into this wildness many failed to make it home. Only a few hardy, slightly deranged trappers and prospectors ever got to know the land well before the area became a national park. Prior to the park, difficult access and de-cidedly aggressive tribes along the Rocky Mountain Front kept all but the most determined white men at bay. Ambushes, harsh winters, and disease took their toll on these civilized wayfarers, but eventually whiskey and newcomer greed leveled the Blackfeet's hold on the east-ern slide. Railroads, surveyors, and homesteaders com-pleted the destruction of the tribe's untamed life.

In 1910, Glacier's million-plus acres officially became a national park. The opening of the Going-to-the-Sun Road in 1933 opened the park's interior to hordes of tourists who viewed the country through windshields and viewfinders. Less than five percent of the visitors ever see anything but what the highway offers and they rarely spend more than a day here. These facts aren't lost on the grizzlies. In their own way they know what is left to them. The bears rarely go near the highway, preferring to mind their own grizzly business in the secluded, glaciated heartland.

But trails were built—lots of them—and the bears are having a hard time avoiding humans. Grizzlies may not fear people, but they don't get a big kick out of being around them either. Humans rarely know what they're doing in the woods and they get in the way a lot—cutting down trees, starting fires, falling off cliffs, and so forth.

There are not a lot of grizzlies left in the lower 48 states—maybe one thousand overall and at the most three hundred in the park, but with tourists scrambling over deadfalls and boulders at every twist of Siyeh Limestone, confrontations are bound to occur—several attacks each season and a handful of deaths so far. These are small figures considering the fact that Glacier has about two million visitors per year.

Still, the Park Service comes up with statements like the following concerning the bears' intransigent behavior: "... the Park is preparing to take a harder line on any bear that has torn up camps, consumed other than natural food, or simply become overly familiar with humans ... that such bears be trapped and immediately removed." While every man's home is his castle, what was once home to the grizzly in this small part of Montana is his no longer. Tough luck guys. Enjoy the view. Eat a few berries, but leave the tourists alone. They're not too bright, but they spend lots of money—bottom-line wildlife management at its finest.

We shouldered our packs as a light afternoon breeze drifted down from the snowfields above us. Upper Kintla was a couple of miles distant. It took an hour to cover the distance to the lake, bears blooming at every turn. Silver-tipped ones, brown ones, mangy ones. Alone or in groups of ten. Take your pick. It was a grizzly blast at the Upper Kintla Trail Bar and Grill. We had cameras (good ones at that), but didn't bother exposing any film. The photos wouldn't have turned out and besides, none of this was happening anyway. Anne talked freely with the bears and they just as freely ignored her.

The mountains were magnificent as usual. We were the only ones at Upper Kintla which now reflected the sky in full sunset, the air dead still.

Several young grizzlies were slapping fish (cutthroats, bull trout?) out of the lake and onto a gravel bar not far from us, just a casual evening meal at the local pond. Fishing's easy if you are a member in good standing in this old-line, well-respected club.

We caught a few small cutthroats on Woolly Worms in deep water off a rocky point at what seemed a polite distance of several hundred yards away from the fishing bears. Then we cooked the fish over a small fire and washed them down with gulps of nonpurified Upper Kintla water (after dealing with about three hundred grizzlies, the threat of *Giardia* seemed a small cross to bear).

We lay down on our sleeping bags under a sky riddled with stars, bears crashing in the woods all around us. Fish by the thousands broke the surface of the water and splashed back. The fire eventually went out. We eventually fell asleep, and the next day was already lurching toward us from beyond the mountains in the east.

The myriad freestone streams and small rivers that flow out of the Whitefish, Swan, Salish, Livingston, Flathead, and Mission mountains feature sufficient variety for any small-stream aficionado. These ice-cold flows are home to some of the last remaining pure-strain populations of westslope cutthroat trout. Rainbows and hybrids of the two species are abundant, as are brook trout and mountain whitefish. There are also bull trout.

These populations, with the exception of the brookies, can be either fluvial (living entirely in a river) or adfluvial (migrating from a lake to spawn in a stream). The migratory trout are on average substantially larger than the stream residents, but when they are on their spawning runs they take a dry fly with substantially less enthusiasm than a creek-dwelling fish. Rainbows typically spawn in the spring, which can be from February through late July depending on the strain of trout and the stream. Because of this some of the best action for the crimson-stained trout occurs before the opening of the general season on the third Saturday in May. Prior to the opener fly fishers must concentrate their efforts on open lakes or any of the many rivers that are open all year.

Cutthroat seem to spawn a bit later. I've seen them on redds in August in one mountain lake, so some delightful fishing is also legal. Several streams in the Whitefish Range empty into Lake Koocanusa, a huge reservoir operated strictly for power generation by those fun-loving folks at the Army Corps of Engineers—a thoughtful bunch who really care about our public lands. Koocanusa resembles a filthy, fly-infested bathtub during the intense drawdowns of late summer. Still, large cutthroat and rainbow trout move out of the reservoir, running many miles upstream, first through open fields and sere hills of wild grasses, then up into fast-flowing, boulder pocket water to still smaller tributaries hidden far back in the timbered mountains. The tiny streams, you can jump across them, hold pure water and clean gravels of the perfect size for redd construction. I fish for these trout first.

A short, light rod is a perfect choice for this water, light enough to be sporting, short enough to cast a line well in close quarters, and strong enough to turn a feisty trout that has ideas other than coming meekly to hand. I vacillate between a one ounce 6½-foot two-weight rod, a 7½-foot one-weight, and a 7-foot, 9-inch two-weight. The selection is based on whim as much as anything, but the little one-ounce rod is a joy to work, with far more zip than one might think. Leaders are kept short, seven or eight feet tapered to 5X. The fish rarely top fifteen inches and average slightly over a foot. After experimenting with countless patterns, I've settled on a gray Elk

Hair Caddis. The pattern clearly takes more and larger trout than any other I've tried. Who knows why. The spawning trout are most often found at the base of small waterfalls and below narrow spouts of water squeezing between two rocks. The hydraulics of the current in these locations give a slight boost to the trout when they attempt to leap up to the next pool. Every advantage, no matter how small, helps. Watching a twelve-inch or on rare occasions an eighteen-inch cutthroat rocket clear of water, land on the lip of the falls, then wriggle to a secure hold in the calm of the pool is a wild sight. At the height of a run I've spent hours observing the fish struggle upstream, driven by the compulsion to replicate their own kind. It is easy to forget to cast a fly. The fishing for migratory trout begins in June after runoff and lasts for a few weeks, past the middle of July.

From then until early September these streams provide wonderful dry fly fishing for native westslope cutthroat trout. I'll fish every day for weeks on these little waters only minutes from home. The fish rise all day whether the sky is clear, bright, hot, or overcast. Cutthroat are joyous fish taking flies with unrestrained enthusiasm. Working a couple of miles of water is bliss. As on the Flathead Reservation, the only equipment required is jeans, tennis shoes, a few flies, and perhaps a light daypack with a sandwich and an apple. Kneeling I drink the water from these streams from a cupped hand in a form of supplication to the universal powers, I suppose. The cutthroat are hanging out in the smallest sanctuaries imaginable. Dapping a fly alongside a slight crease in the pulsing current next to a deadfall brings not one but several trout out from cover in a carefree downstream chase as the fly zips by. The fish leap and snap at the bug. It is not necessary to set the hook, doing so just results in the small fish being flipped from the river over my head like miniature tuna-boat fishing.

Long emerald pools formed behind logjams or along sweeping curves in the stream produce six, seven, eight fish. Bang. Bang. Bang. Cast to that seam. Whip the caddis beneath that forked branch. Bounce it between the limbs of that fallen fir. The cutthroat are there and they're eager. There is no way I'll ever tire of this fishing. Every cast is different, requiring a quick read that factors in current, distance, prime holding water, stealth, and drift. Working these streams compared to casting weighted Buggers for big-time autumn browns is like steering a Triumph Spitfire through the twists and turns of a country lane at 70 mph as opposed to powering a Ford Ranger three-quarter-ton pickup down the Inter-state at 90. I love both types of fishing and will never get enough of either, or any other fly fishing for that matter.

By early September the days are growing notice-ably shorter and cooler. The undergrowth is now aflame with rust, scarlet, orange, yellow, and purple. The aspen are hinting at the fall gold to follow. Rose hips are hot-red and fat, bending the limbs toward the ground. There are officially three weeks of summer left, but the stream fishing for the cutthroat and other species is finished. A stretch that produced forty trout earlier now yields per-haps three. The fish have either slipped back downstream to overwinter in the deep safety of the lakes or have moved into sheltered holding areas within the stream course. By now I'll have devoted forty to fifty days wading these streams, much of the time spent sitting on large rocks or downed trees watching the shifting currents, listening to the air move through the pines, maybe spotting an elk or a group of whitetails gliding silently through the trees. The banks are full of tracks of these animals along with those from bears, cats, kingfishers, and ravens.

This is fly fishing in its sweet, pure essence. The passing of another season is sad, lonely, reminiscent of shooting upland birds. With each crisp, blue-sky September I'm increasingly aware that I'll have one less year of fishing. How many are left for me? I wonder.

The high country lakes truly shine in early September. After Labor Day most visitors have left the state, children are back in school, and many anglers have turned their attentions to hunting. The air is crisp and the light shines like expensive crystal held to a flickering candle. Aspen are turning as are larch at the higher elevations. The undergrowth, huckleberry bushes, and alder are a riot of color. Unfished in autumn are the small, deep, cold lakes hidden in slight depressions carved by retreating ice fields thousands of years ago or turquoise waters backed against the sheer walls of massive glacial cirques. Actually many go unvisited for years on end due to their abundance, remoteness, and the presence of bears. "So much water to fish, so little time," the boys down at the local fly shop are heard to say.

One lake stands above all others. It is not especially beautiful though it lies in wild country. The fish are not exceptionally large nor is the water easily accessible. What draws me here is the large number of native cutthroat. Westslope cutthroat are fat, firm, and colorful. As far as I can determine no one else fishes here, which makes it even more attractive. Anyone other than a good friend constitutes an unacceptable intrusion. Crowds and fishing do not mix well in my estimation. The water lies several miles beyond a gate across an old logging road and that scares off most people, though I occasionally see the tracks of mountain bikes. Fresh droppings from grizzlies, elk, deer, and moose are more common. Much of the country has been clear-cut, but is coming back slowly. Dark fir forest guards all but the southern shore which gives way to young larch and spruce. Beaver activity some years past raised the lake a couple of feet and flooded a good deal of treed shoreline. The dead gray snags and rust-colored limbs create superb habitat for the cutthroat. The trout hold in the cover right beneath the surface, rising easily to the surface or inches below to feed.

I can walk in on what's left of the rocky road in less than two hours, toting with me a small pack raft, three-weight rod, related equipment, and some food and beverage. The road is littered with cracked and broken rock fallen from overhanging cliffs. Brush, grass, and small trees have taken over much of the level surface. Where the road begins a series of switchbacks on its way to the lake, tag alder and deadfalls would make travel by four-wheel drive virtually impossible. Bear vibes rattle through the air. Fresh scat is common, some so new that my cousin Steve refers to the piles as "steamers." For some reason bears prefer elimination on logging roads. If they used other portions of the woods and mountains with similar zest, a conservative estimate of their numbers in the northern Continental Divide ecosystem would be one hundred thousand instead of the accepted figure of about one thousand. I can visualize a half-ton griz hunched in the middle of the road surveying his domain with suzerain authority, the sun rising over the distant peaks of Glacier casting a natural spotlight on the stately bruin engaged in morning ritual. Quite a sight, I'm sure.

The sound of running water betrays the presence of the lake. A small stream runs through dense ground cover. Tiny trout live here. At the outlet I inflate the raft, assemble the kayaklike paddle and the rod, and pray that whatever fate awaits me in this flimsy vessel is a condign one.

There is no breeze. The lake's surface is smooth except for the hundreds of riseforms created by the feeding trout. When I first fished this water several years back the fish averaged less than a foot, now they are close to fifteen inches and over a pound, making this one of the most productive cutthroat trout lakes in this part of the country. The fish are everywhere in this twenty-acre by at most ten-foot-deep pond. Small springs bubble up through the mud and aquatic grass providing oxygen and preventing the water from freezing solid during winter when temperatures drop to fifty below and snow piles up to depths of twenty or more feet.

Small dries like midges and *Baetis* and Tricos take fish consistently here. Cutthroat take these flies readily. Still, I prefer a soft-hackled fly tied with mottled partridge feather and orange silk wound with thin gold wire.

Casts of fifty feet that are allowed to sink a foot or two then retrieved slowly and sporadically are too much for the trout to resist. I use the conjunction of the leader and the yellow line as an indicator. The slightest movement away from the raft means a fish. I merely lift the rod to drive the hook home and the cutthroat respond with splashing acrobatics and spirited, determined head-shaking runs. The fish always look like they are in spawning colors—bright orange blending to burning scarlet along their bellies and lower flanks and gill plates; dark backs; yellows or grapefruit pinks on the fins; and hundreds of black spots. These beautiful fish are among my favorites because of their spectacular appearance, their native wildness, and behavior that suggests that westslope cutthroat trout are the true sybarites of the salmonid clan. They appear to swim and feed as much out of joy as necessity.

Within thirty minutes I've caught and released close to a dozen. The height of the sun indicates noon or later. The next three trout I keep. On shore I build a fire of sticks and small limbs and melt butter in a cast iron frying pan (added weight but worth the monumental gain in aesthetics and cooking quality). Then I pop the cork from a bottle of Sauvignon blanc chilling in a small trickle that seeps from the ground above a bed of bright green moss. The trout have been cleaned, guts and gills removed, heads left on. They sizzle in the pan. I tear some fresh sourdough French bread into pieces and place it on a plate. The fish cook quickly, and I pour the butter over their sides, then squeeze a wedge of lemon on top of this, and add a bit of salt and pepper to complete the preparations. The fire is down to coals and I toss some more sticks on. They leap into flame, keeping me company while I eat. This is the way trout should be consumed. Fresh and tasting of the butter and lemon, and tannin of their home water. The bread soaks up the butter and juice and tastes pretty damn good, too. The cold wine is more than all right.

The sound of the sipping trout and some three-toed woodpeckers in the trees behind me is perfect music. A raven slides by, drawn by the smell of the cooking. The bird croaks twice and wheels around in the air that rushes over its wings in an audible "whoosh." One more quick look and the black creature sails rapidly over the trees, out of sight.

There is time for a few more fish and another hour yields over twenty. Then it is time to pack. The sun is almost behind the mountains in the west. The walk back will be a brisk one; it is spooky on the old road in the night with all the bears around. Near dark I reach the truck. The drive home takes almost two hours, but the pace is relaxed, easy. Another fine day playing in the mountains.

If anyone ever bothered to look with any diligence at the fir tree behind me, they would be amazed at what they would find: an exotic collection of flies draped on the tree's limbs as though in preparation for a preternatural celebration of the yuletide by a sect of practicing fly fishing ascetics. Suspended by varying lengths of tippet material or embedded in the resin-rich limbs were Blue Charms, Gold-Ribbed Hare's Ear Nymphs, Mickey Finns, Yuk Bugs, Elk Hair Caddis, Red Serendipitys, a Jock Scott, an Orange Double Humpy, and a brace of olive Woolly Buggers. This complemented an assortment of similarly esoteric dimensions that I'd deposited in a casting frenzy last year while fishing with my sister Anne. Something about this place called for a ritualistic flinging of every exotic, bizarre, and inappropriate pattern in the vest. That most of these patterns found their way into the seductive arms of the pine at my back seemed proper in the thin alpine air.

This rocky point jutting into water cold enough that it should have been frozen was called Hidden Lake and it was in Glacier Park. This was a perfect location for spotting cruising Yellowstone cutthroat. They glided silently by perhaps thirty-five to forty feet from shore, an easy cast except for the fir trees, one in particular, less than twenty-five feet behind me. For a cast to be effective, for the fly to reach the feeding trout, the line must be jerked off the water and then flung at an angle of greater than sixty degrees into the air, then pitched forward and flattened out into a smooth approach with a downward scooping motion of the elbow coordinated with a sudden flexing of the knees. Observed from a distance the procedure probably resembled someone experiencing cardiac arrest or worse. My success rate was abysmal, but the proximity of so many willing Yellowstone cutthroat was irresistible, intoxicating. This is one of the few lakes in the region containing the species. East of the Divide they are the most common mountain trout, but not on the west slope. The fact that I had tied the flies and in doing so had partially offset the cost of the lost patterns was slight consolation. So far I'd lost more than a dozen and taken three trout.

The first fish I hooked was twenty inches, just barely if I pulled on the tail fin. Wide-bodied but not chunky. Golden in overall color with a hint of a red band and a wisp of bluish-purple parr markings. The black spots were large and scattered parsimoniously along the tail and back. The fish more closely resembled golden trout than westslope cutthroat. They were beautiful, riding like suspended precious-metal ingots in the sapphire water, but they fought with the zest of a road-killed gopher. They struck, shook their heads once or twice in a perfunctory manner, then allowed themselves to be reeled in ignominiously. When removing the hook, one looked up with an expression that seemed to say, "Hey! This is a national park and they don't pay me enough to look beautiful and fight, too. At least it's a job and I'm not out collecting welfare somewhere." Any resemblance between these gorgeous pretenders and river-run rainbows was accidental.

Yellowstones fight with a good deal more flare and anger in the lakes of the Beartooths or the Gallatin Range. Perhaps being so far from home broke their spirit, sapped their strength. But they were an eyeful and so was this unspoiled lake nestled in a small valley beneath towering peaks and snowfields less than four miles from the visitor center at Logan Pass. Late September was a fine time to fish here. The cattlelike herds of windshield tourists had mostly departed. The backcountry was quiet, isolated. I had the water to myself. Marmots whistled back and forth in the rocks and hanging gardens far above. Fall color was resplendent, coordinating nicely with an azure sky. Designer landscaping Glacier style.

The other two trout were an inch or two less than the magic twenty-inch barrier and just as bright as their larger relation. One or two Yellowstones would pass by my station at regular intervals of about fifteen minutes. When the flies weren't tangling in the fir and were actually landing in front of the trout, the fishing was easy. A quick tug on the line, a hint of flash, and the cutthroat raced for the nymphs, streamers, and dries with wide-open jaws flashing white in the diamond water. Not one of them fought like its life depended on the outcome of the struggle (which well it could have). The rod would flex once or twice and then remain bowed with the resistance of the trout as I wound them in to shore. They were still fun to catch and to watch as they swam nonchalantly before me. They were an excellent excuse to drive up here and make the steep hike up and down the mountainside along a trail of several thousand switchbacks.

This country is marked by dramatic changes in elevation. Even supposedly benign trails offer a fair amount of exposure as they cling to the sides of rock walls. Suddenly rounding a bend and seeing the world fall away abruptly for a thousand feet or more is not a pleasant experience. One summer when cousin Steve was flying all around the West accumulating hours toward some commercial rating, he took Jack, Elizabeth, and myself on a flight over the park. Legally aircraft are supposed to stay at least two thousand feet above the highest land elevation in a given area. This flight may have violated this dictum as the twin-engine Beech angled toward the peaks before banking sharply then leveling off to soar over saddles in the mountains and just above the crevassed, blue-white fields of receding glaciers. The track into Hidden looked like a dirty tan thread. The lake was a dark blue surrounded by stark peaks—Clements, Reynolds—of gray and black rock. We rode a thermal over Gunsight Pass and Sperry, Jackson, Blackfoot, and Pumpelly glaciers, then sailed across the Middle Fork valley and into the Bob Marshall Wilderness complex. The kids enjoyed the wind-standing turns and rapid drops through space. I enjoyed the view. Steve laughed often. That was the first time I'd flown literally between the mountains in my home country. I gained a much better overall knowledge of the lay of the land and the immense forces that formed the peaks and valleys. Walking through the country is one form of awareness. Gliding above the land is another. Steve's love of flying was now understandable.

There was another September, one of my first in this part of the park, during midweek when very few vehicles were parked at the Logan Pass lot. After a mile of hiking on the wide boardwalk, I had the country to myself. Again the marmots whistled to each other, their calls slicing through the still air. Late-blooming ground cover brightened the trip. The steppes were turning from green to yellow, orange, and brown. A group of mountain goats was grazing among some juniper at the lake's overlook. The animals see so many people, are photographed and fed (in contravention of park regulations) so often, that they are borderline tame, unless a nanny perceives a human threat to her kids. Then that person is in for a charge, one with horns and sharp hooves. My money is always on the goats. They ignored my passing.

After another forty minutes of hiking, I was casting to the cutthroat, this time near the outlet while standing in shallow water along a gravel shore. Almost everyone I've spoken to concerning the fishing here claims that the trout are difficult to catch, elusive, and frustrating. My experience has been otherwise. Any pattern presented well in front of the Yellowstone cutthroats, far enough away to avoid spooking the fish when the fly lands on the water, takes trout. A slight strip that barely wiggles the nymph, streamer, or dry draws the trout's attention. They come steadily to the pattern and take with a downward, sideways turn of their heads. When turned loose, the fish never race off for shelter. They slide down below the surface a few feet and resume their unconcerned, leisurely tour of the shoreline.

THE
SWEET SEASON
ARRIVES

THE
SWEET SEASON
ARRIVES

How could I have ignored a stream of this caliber so close to home? Less than a three-hour drive from Whitefish flows one (actually there are dozens) of the finest rivers in the country. Today the water has never fished better. Aspens, cottonwoods, and larch display the intense gold, yellow, and orange of early October. Rainbows are feeding in pods, stacked up in lines along prime runs, or racing about the riffles gulping fall caddis. A #14 light-brown Elk Hair with an orange chenille body never has an opportunity to ride more than a few feet of the river before it is swallowed by one of the trout. In this stream the fish are brightly tinted with red, purple, aquamarine, and silver. They are strong fish that know how to use the current, how to turn their flanks into the flow for maximum resistance—fish that will leap several times in succession out of anger, frustration, and a desire to snap the tippet. There are miles and miles of water to cast over, filled with rising trout. Two days, three days, a week is not enough time. The intensity of autumn rides in on warm breezes that glide down the canyon, rustling and pulling dry leaves from the trees. The surface of the river is littered with them, their pointed shapes spinning and sliding downstream to the Clark Fork River thirty miles distant. There is absolutely no one here. It would be impossible to improve on this setting.

And that is why fall fly fishing is my favorite, a time of the season when work, social niceties (those I infrequently practice), and other responsibilities are pushed aside. Even the most famous of Montana's rivers are uncrowded. The summer tourist frenzy is over and people are smiling, genuinely friendly again. The waitress at a restaurant in Choteau asks where I'm headed and offers some suggestions about chasing browns and hunting Hungarian partridge. Others in the place offer further advice. Store owners in West Yellowstone are helpful, relaxed. The highways are almost safe to drive. The browns are starting to move in all the major streams and in many lesser ones that can hold their own when it comes to good fishing. Brook trout are lighting up in the beaver ponds. Rainbows and cutthroat are feeding aggressively everywhere. Dries, streamers, wet flies, nymphs—take your pick. They all work. The largest browns I've ever taken have come from autumn rivers. The same holds true in stillwater for brook trout.

From the first day of fall through about the last week in October the fishing improves dramatically (from already lofty standards). The days are usually clear and cold with frost in the mornings warming sometimes into the seventies by three o'clock. Sunset is around seven. My family understands that my desire, my need, to chase trout at this time is an unrestrained, out-of-control passion. They do not wish to be around me if for some reason I am housebound. Winter is bad enough, they say. So I pile up the miles running from river to stream to isolated lake. The pickup is stuffed with camping and fishing gear. A shotgun or two lies behind the seat.

Sometimes another twisted soul joins me on the trip. Those who understand the road like Talia and Jones and a few others make a special trip that much better. Fishing with an honest, straightforward friend, sharing food and later whiskey around a bright fire in the evening, planning the next day's fishing and bird hunting, that is special stuff and a person hangs onto friends with those qualities. They are not easy to find. Often someone who sounded eager and willing over the phone turns out to be a simpering whiner who must be jettisoned as soon as possible. Fortunately their kind are easily spotted. These types of mistakes are not to be repeated.

The boxes of Woolly Buggers, Blue-Winged Olives, Elk Hair Caddis, and other patterns along with a half dozen or so rods, reels, and spare spools have been cleaned and packed. It is time to leave. Lynda waves goodbye knowing I'll be much calmer when I return. Let the chase begin.

I drained off the last two inches of beer in the Carta Blanca bottle as a burrito stuffed with refried beans, salsa, and jalapeño peppers splattered against the knotty pine paneling behind me. Something was seriously wrong here. What, I wasn't sure. I peered through the cigar smoke at a cluster of mustaches buried under sombreros. They were grouped around a five-gallon jug of mescal.

Where were the trout? Where was northwestern Montana? For that matter, where's the first tee and what's the course record? Things were out of control and I was afraid. The smell of panic swirled around my stool, a scent sure to trigger a frenzy of mustachioed violence. Terror made me brave. I ordered another beer in a calm voice. A long drink of the cold, bubbling liquid soothed my nerves. Control returned as another burrito and some shrimp splashed across the front of a nonworking television set behind the bar. Three days ago I was fishing for westslope cutthroat trout, enjoying the serenity of the North Fork. That was gone now. The trip had degenerated into a nightmare of fermented cactus juice and twisted behavior.

This was awful beyond comprehension.

My companion (of extremely shaky mental assembly) had disappeared with one of the natives, guzzling tequila in a '54 Chevy pickup.

Just this afternoon we had enjoyed some pleasant fly fishing for ten- to twelve-inch trout on Red Meadow Creek just a few miles northwest of here. Where's here you might ask? On the map it is Polebridge, Montana, and in graphic specificity, the Northern Lights Lunatic Fringe Emporium. About as far north as you can go in the state without running into crazed Canadians on their home turf.

The fishing was slow in the late-September heat, but a few trout rose to an imitation hopper drifted along the edges of the many logjams and undercut banks where the creek wandered through an old burn and the site of some logging several decades ago—open country with beat-up mountains dominating the horizon. We were oblivious to the foul fate lurking in the approaching twilight.

A bullet blasted through a picture window, breaking several bottles of cheap wine that were collecting an impressive amount of dust on a shelf behind the bar. The tape player (powered by a gasoline generator chugging away out back) broke into "The Lonely Bulls" and the sombreros unleashed a spirited chorus of "Ole's" punctuated by gunfire. I lit a Camel straight and inhaled deeply. The nicotine made me dizzy.

I had had glimmerings of an ill-defined craziness on earlier trips to this region … suggestions of aberrant behavior peaking around corners of the club. But this … this sordid display of hedonism was too much. The Northern Lights' annual Autumn Mexican Soireé was fiendishly out of control. Wild women, gunplay, flying food, alcohol in mad profusion—no, this wasn't trout fishing in America. This was over the edge in Guadalajara, Montana.

An incident yesterday should have been a warning, but the tranquil pace of the area had put my synapses to sleep. We were fishing the upper reaches of the North Fork River, an emerald-colored stream with a few big fish that will rise to the occasion with the proper stimulation (this holds true for many of us). Returning to our truck at the end of the day, we spotted a man leaning on the hood. He was sporting hip waders, a battered, greasy Abercrombie & Fitch (the label was stuck to the fleece patch) fishing vest, a leather flying helmet with goggles shoved rakishly atop his head, and most importantly to us, a 9mm pistol. A sardonic smile revealed a pair of front uppers with inlays of gold crosses. "We're through for sure this time," I thought. Pointing the weapon in my direction, he asked if we always trespassed when we fished (it turned out that we were on National Forest, a minor consideration at the time). We both apologized for our transgressions and that warmed the guy's heart.

For what seemed like several days we were regaled with tales of wild dogs led by a giant wolf, black bears that had lost their fear of humans and drove Buicks, manic charging deer that had to be beaten back with the butt of a fly rod, and other tales of madness. Visions of the Posse Comitatus marauded through our brains as horseflies buzzed around us in the late afternoon glow.

After several deft maneuvers we were finally inside the cab of the truck. Luck was with us. The engine started. As I let out the clutch, our friend stuck his face inside and asked, "Are either of you fellas German?"

"Damn straight," we replied.

"Thought so," the old face chuckled. "That's something to be proud of." This point was hammered home with a vicious banging of the 9mm's muzzle on the base of our truck's antenna. So much for the acoustic joys of the Lethbridge AM Radio Polka Hour on the way back to our campsite. As we rounded the bend in high-speed escape, the old man's reflection shimmered in the side mirror, yellow-gray dust boiling around his waders.

An excellent New York strip steak plucked from the dark recesses of our mouldy cooler, a drink or two, and a night sky filled with meteors blocked out the day's dangerous message. We headed over to the Northern Lights for a nightcap.

It was now much later, perhaps too late. A dark-haired woman with a grizzly bear claw hanging from one ear was dancing around a hat on the quarter pool table. A large bull trout (the last of its kind?) mounted on the wall was sporting bandoliers and a crooked, smoldering cigar (Honduran?). The soireé was in full swing in the acrid atmosphere.

Jack, the bar's owner, staggered into view.

"Nice party," I said.

He tripped over something behind the bar (a body?), mumbled something about "Monopoly money" and headed for the floor. I never saw him again.

"Are you German? I thought so. You know, that's something to be proud of."

I looked to my left and there was my wilderness Posse Comitatus friend in full regalia—helmet, fishing vest, hip-waders covered with brown dust, and the 9mm pistol resting on the bar. Looking to see who the guy was talking to, I should have guessed. It was his slightly distorted reflection in the mirror. Par for the course around here.

The party wound into high gear, tightly wrapping back on itself in layers of frenetic lunacy. I eventually lost track of things, sliding slowly backwards in a lazy arc, coming to rest in two bounces on the floor next to the beer cooler, dead to the "south of the border" din.

Daybreak. The sound of the generator kicking on woke me. I stood up, slowly, and looked around. The place was empty and spotless. No burritos sliding down walls. No sweet smell of mescal. No cigar smoke. Even the fish on the wall was back to normal. No bandoliers or stinking cigar.

The front door was open. I walked out to the truck and found my friend curled up in his sleeping bag on the seat. The town was deserted. Ours was the only vehicle parked on "main" street. Glacier Park was bathed in the fresh sunlight, a beautiful day brewing in northwest Montana.

My buddy sat up, looked around to get his bearings and asked, "Where we goin' fishin' today?"

If he wasn't fazed by last night's activities, neither was I.

"Let's try Red Meadow again, after some coffee."

The memory of the evening's debacle was fading fast and with a cup or two of strong, black java, along with a few eggs, the experience might not end up being all bad. Breakfast at a small roadside joint way down the road in bucolic Columbia Falls was filling. The fishing promised to be good.

I went to the cash register up front to pay our bill. Reaching into my jeans for some loose change, something felt strange, sticky. Withdrawing my hand, I saw, as though from a great distance, a wad of pesos and a couple of salsa-smeared shrimp.

"We're through," I thought one more time.

But a good sport plays them where they lie.

Friends and I were chasing trout in the Cascade River near its junction with Stoney Creek, a solid twenty miles from Banff, Alberta, Canada, and its gift stores purveying overpriced curios, hotels offering overpriced rooms, restaurants serving overpriced food, and thoroughfares filled with hordes of visitors from the Pacific Rim. The great Canadian come-on eagerly proclaiming what a bargain the country was for those of us living in the U.S. because of the favorable exchange rate was a con, a Chamber of Commerce pitch promoted by greedy PR types eager for quick bucks. It was apparently working. Even in late September the town was crawling with tourists, a far cry from a stay twenty years ago when we cross-country skied to a downtown bar to hear a good rock band and drink lots of Jack Daniels. Banff had gone belly up beneath the somber face of the Canadian Rockies. The country back here was pretty, though, but not really wild like Glacier or the Rocky Mountain Front.

    This was the second day of a five-day pack trip that took us on a loop through spectacular country that had unfortunately been carved up with roads designed to facilitate the outfitter's supply regime. The fifty-mile trip through dark pine forest, over tundralike meadows, alongside precipitous drop-offs, and along free-flowing streams was a disappointment. The country was tamed, commercialized, and our guides and packers were bored with their work, along only for the paycheck. The first day had been a long one. Our initial attempts at travel from the trailhead at Mt. Norquay Ski Area had been repelled by a large number of trees down across the trail, felled during a recent wind and snow storm. While we waited, wranglers drove back into town to retrieve a chainsaw. We gave the lead logger-wrangler a fifteen-

minute headstart to clear the obstructions before lethar-
gically striking out one more time. The horses' hooves
clattered along the rocky trail as we worked our way
through forest and up onto the barren, windswept plateau of Elk Summit. Wet snow was driven into my face by
a mean north wind. Rain, sleet, and fog filled the gap left
by the soon-departed snow squall. The mountains vanished from view. The trail turned ugly, rough, and
potholed as we started down beside a small stream that
led to the first night's camp. The going was treacherous
and one of the horses hung up. The young rider was
swiftly and brutally reduced to tears by the surly lead
wrangler who yelled and cursed the child's inability to
extricate the terrified animal from the mud and exposed
roots.

"Lighten up on her, Ace," I yelled, the blood
pounding up into my head.

"I'm boss of this outfit," the old goat snarled.

"How nice for you. Take your anger out on someone else, buddy."

"Mind your own business and do as you're told,"
he hissed.

The string of riders grew dead silent—high noon
in a raging blizzard at the Banff coral.

"Kiss my ass, fella," I said as he came toward me
with a nasty, red-eyed look. "Montana writer killed by
irate wrangler in Canadian Rockies." I could see the
headline clearly. But fate intervened in the form of an
actor of minor but generous talent along for the ride
during a filming break in nearby Calgary.

"Let it go. You freed her horse. We're all cold and
tired. Come on. Drop it," he urged. The wrangler took

the advice and we resumed our journey. The actor flicked a swift grin and a quick thumbs-up my way, but I was persona non grata with the trail crew for the remainder of the happy cruise. What the hell; boredom breeds misbehavior in the hot-headed. This far in the only choice was to make the best of a lifeless, grim operation, and there were country and trout ahead.

The lights of camp were a welcome sight as was my tent. I stowed the gear, downed a couple of shots of bourbon, and wandered to the cook tent for dinner, fleeing as soon as the sing-along progressed to full wail. The sound of howling coyotes kicked up on the slopes surrounding camp. Returning to the tent, I smoked cigarettes and drank more bourbon with the actor and another guy. The sky cleared and the stars came out. Elk bugled back and forth in the mountains above, a feral, primitive sound. The situation seemed a little better in the dark. I could handle four more days of this.

Perhaps from some sense of sympathy, day two was a layover day. While the majority of the party that numbered well over twenty (we'd all been told while booking the ride that the size of the group would be eight or less) opted for a day trip that took them high into the surrounding peaks, several of us spent the time fishing the river for westslope cutthroat and bull trout. The cutthroat here had fewer but larger spots than those found in the Flathead. Other than that, they were identical to the eye. I placed an immediately suspect reputation as a fly fisher on the line. My new friends—we were now bonded by a shared feeling of being scammed and a growing anger fueled by the condescending, moody attitude of the staff—assumed that I could catch trout on demand.

"Oh, you make your living writing about fishing," they said smiling wickedly. "Well, you must be awfully good. We'll follow you around and pick up some pointers." This was quickly followed by my hanging up the first cast in a nearby tree (skills learned at Hidden Lake die a hard, ugly death), breaking off on a pile of logs, and snagging one of my now not-so-eager companions. I was ready for the glitz of the show circuit. Stand back. Holt's here and ready to cast.

They were polite souls and smiled again saying, "We think we'll move upstream and try our luck a little. Let you have some time to yourself. See you back at camp." I was left alone, fly rod clutched in one hand, unlit cigar in another. The daypack held several beers and a chunk of cheddar cheese I'd cadged from the kitchen stores while the cook was taking a belt of blackberry brandy on the sly. Never kid a kidder I told her later as we killed a fresh bottle of the sweet stuff while the rest of the hapless crew slogged their way through an interminable sing-along later that evening that made watching back-to-back-to-back reruns of the Lawrence Welk Show seem positively rapturous.

At any rate, I relished the solitude after too many hours lurching in a saddle of a surly horse that did as it pleased. Heading upriver a quarter mile or so, I began working likely looking pocket water with a #6 Black-Nosed Dace. The Cascade is not big water, maybe forty feet wide, but the stream is loaded with perfect habitat for cutthroat—plunge pools, brushy banks, deep runs, and logjams. Working each likely spot in the river for several hundred yards turned a dozen trout up to fourteen inches. One bull trout (you are still allowed to catch them in Alberta) took and put up a strong subsurface fight before being dragged to shore. Around twenty inches, dull silver and washed-out green, the char was a faded replica of its Montana relations. Perhaps this was due to the time of year or the natural characteristics of the water. Who knew? I turned the fish loose and cast some more without much enthusiasm.

The landscape was beautifully wild and the river was a gem with plenty of fish. But the blatant commercialism of the outfitter, the domestication of truly splendid country, and the surly crew had all created a decidedly blue mood. Perhaps some of that brandy would help, I thought, and went looking for the cook. I think I liked her, at least as long as the "berry" held up.

On the way back I noticed small fall caddis whirring above the stream and near the bushes. Turning rocks revealed plenty of larvae and some stonefly nymphs. The stream, while sterile by Missouri River standards, certainly contained enough bugs to grow trout. I'd try some nymphing tomorrow evening at the next joyous camp.

My new friends returned to the mess tent as the cook and I drained the bottle of brandy. I felt better and I was eagerly awaiting the creative efforts of the chef this evening. The returning bunch had taken a number of trout on spinners, bringing several fat ones back for dinner. The cook said she'd fry them up as a side dish for the baked ham.

The trip progressed through the mountains with the dudes gradually sinking into a mood of lassitude broken only by outbreaks of turpitude among the crew, as they constantly bickered among themselves over the building of lunchtime fires and tending the stock. I am convinced that had this trip lasted a week, people would have died. I stayed at the end of the string during the day, minding my own business and sharing an occasional pop of either my bourbon or the actor's Glenlivet. Of such moments are memories made. The next three nights we arrived so late in camp that fishing was impossible. The routine was unpacking, eating, more hideous singing for some, whiskey and nicotine for the actor and me, and then sleep.

"How'd you get trapped on this trip, John?"

"I thought it would be fun. I wanted to see the country."

"Me, too. Boy were we wrong on that one," the actor said as he passed the bottle.

The next to the last day was the most interesting. After a sedate climb along a gradual divide, we crossed a creek and suddenly were heading almost straight up a narrow ridge. My horse was puffing with the exertion. To either side the earth dropped away for hundreds of feet. One look and my eyes fixed on the bobbing mane of my mount. I could not see the trail. The animal's belly was too wide, nothing but space. At each switchback we appeared to hang, suspended out in dizzying nothingness, an instant away from a lethal free fall. Life was reduced to faith in a cantankerous sixteen-year-old horse. God this was fun.

Then we broke out onto a wide plateau called Forty Mile Summit. Solid land was below me, a most welcome sight. All around rugged blue, purple, and white-capped mountains dominated the horizon. Pines grew down to the edge of a meadow now covered in a couple of feet of fresh snow. This was truly magnificent country that made me temporarily forget the acrophobia of a few minutes ago and the long miasma of the dark ride. I'd love to come here with friends on our own horses if regulations allowed. They probably didn't. But that view, the few minutes of bliss is with me today. Nowhere have I looked upon better country.

The next morning I awoke to another foot of snow. The ride back to Mt. Norquay was ten miles of slippery, muddy trail. A steady drizzle hounded our escape. Near the end, our fearless leader pulled up, had us form a semicircle, and then proceeded to launch into a forty-minute diatribe about what a "great group" we'd been (I'm not kidding) and how people like us made his "time in the mountains special." A member of the crew rode up and turned off a small switch located just beneath the leader's left ear. We finished the ride in sodden silence.

Back in Banff, the actor and I, after long, hot showers and a change into fresh clothes hit the town hard. We ate rare steaks, swilled expensive wine, then drank gallons of beer at a saloon.

Around 1:00 a.m. our leader and his crew showed up quite drunk. I walked by saying "Goodbye."

The wrangler barked a "Screw off."

The next morning I stopped and fished the Elk River outside of Ferni near the U.S.-Canadian border halfway through the drive back to the real world. A strong hatch of large, fall caddis was coming off and I turned a number of trout of a couple of pounds and a few larger. The river was only a few hours from home and I made a mental note to spend more time here next year.

Clearing customs and driving down Highway 93 past Eureka on my way back to Whitefish was nice. It would be good to get home and hug the family.

Each year trudging up to this lake seems to get harder, the incline steeper, the distance longer, the air thinner. The last pitch to the water is a scramble through wet, rotting vegetation and low limbs that grab and hold the clumsy pack on my back. The path dissolves into a multitude of game trails that lead off to the most obscure and hard-to-return-from places, like dead-end cliffs, insurmountable rock walls, and swampy meadows of no return. I've been coming here for years in October, the visit an annual rite, a final tour and farewell to the high country before winter clamps down on the mountains. Some may even say that this urge to escape is fueled by my growing misanthropy. Perhaps, but I think the country itself is sufficient inducement. Rupert, my Australian Shepherd, loved this place but he is too old to make the hike anymore. Our youthful golden retriever, Zack, is still too goofy. A grizzly would seem a friend to play with in the inchoate mind of the happy dog. As he so often says with a carefree smile and laughing brown eyes, "It's tough being a retriever." Maybe next year.

Finally clambering over a rock shelf, the twenty-five acre lake comes into view. It is deep, with the rock and snow faces of severe mountains and fields of shattered granite climbing several thousand feet into the sky on the far shore. Small streams of snowmelt pour into the sapphire water. Even from here I spy hundreds of small goldens lying motionless in the water or tipping daintily to the surface to sip a midge. The lake is difficult to find even with a good topo map. I've never seen anyone else here in more than twenty years. Other places in this range of mountains along the east shore of Flathead Lake are overrun with boy scout troops, yupsters doing the politically correct thing on their days off from the yogurt factory, and even the former vice-president Dan Quayle and his sycophantic entourage once or twice a summer. But this place is out of the way. The hike is only seven miles, but I'm hot, tired, and sweaty even in the cool air of autumn at over seven thousand feet above sea level.

The forecast calls for a high pressure system to hold in place for the next week or so, a common occurrence this time of year, so I bagged the tent. Tarp, sleeping pad, and bag are spread on a bed of grass and moss sheltered by igneous rock. A well-used fire ring, it was here the first time I visited, needs some minor repair. The pile of limbs, sticks, and logs I stacked beneath an overhang in the rock last year is still there, dry and ready to burn. I've also brought a small bag of mesquite charcoal to flavor the New York strip steak I'll grill tonight and, I hope, a few goldens tomorrow evening. Pots are filled with lake water for coffee and for soaking silverware, as is a plastic bottle for sipping during the day to avoid dehydration. Food, including cans of jalapeño chili, smoked oysters, a box of Triscuits, some Stilton cheese, tomatoes, Greek olives, pears, lemons, butter, Golden

Sumatran coffee, several bottles of Beck's, a bottle of Jack, a liter of Pouilly Fuisse (for the sauteed trout of course), and a bottle of cognac, is arranged in a tasteful display along a smooth slab of rock. Could it be that the reason the hike seems to grow in difficulty each year is quite possibly connected to the amount of food and drink I lug in?

The stroll in took about three hours. It is now late afternoon and the sun is dipping over the peaks to the southwest. The water is in shadow but the goldens are easily spotted. The four-weight covers sixty feet and an olive Woolly Worm plops lightly in front of a fish of a foot or less. I allow the fly to sink for a couple of feet, then give it slight strips and pauses making the pattern wiggle like a leech or large nymph. The targeted golden races in and snares the fake just ahead of three others. The fish fluoresces at the unexpected sting of the hook, running and shaking in ever-tightening circles in the crystal depths of the lake. Other goldens turn to watch the struggle, unconcerned, unmoved at the possibly dire fate awaiting their brother. I reach down and grab the eye of the fly and lift the trout to me. Yellow-gold on the body with parr markings of deep purple surrounded by green with black spots and milky white tipping on the fins. There is a blush of rose on each gill plate. An absolutely gorgeous trout. There is no other word for this perfection. The trout shoots away on release. I catch several more in an hour's casting. This lake denied its goldens for years until I stumbled upon the olive Woolly Worm. No other bug works, for me at least. Not Hare's Ears, Adams, leeches, Biggs Specials, hoppers, Wulffs (royal and less regal), Prince Nymphs, or Elk Hairs. But the

Woolly Worm in olive, not black or gray or brown, has enticed the finicky goldens into action for fifteen years now.

Back at camp the sticks and dried grass burst into flame with the touch of an Ohio Blue-Tip match. I build a drink with the Jack and some water from the lake in a glass I carry wrapped safely in a towel for the occasion. The steak is rubbed with crushed garlic and some fresh lemon juice. A can of chili is bubbling in a corner of the fire. A few of the oysters on the crackers go nicely with the drink. The olives aren't bad either—sweet, salty, earthy. I make another bourbon and toss the meat on the small grill. Flavorful smoke is soon drifting past me. The steak sizzles and curls along the edges.

Except for the first time in here when I traveled with a college sweety, I've always come back alone or with Rupert. This is my place, one of the few left and I guard its location jealously. Conventional knowledge holds that there is only one lake holding goldens in this narrow mountain range. There are four. Two have names and two do not on most maps. This is one of the latter. There is no indication that anyone has been here since last October. No beer cans, gum wrappers, Styrofoam worm containers, plastic spoons. I've checked the area and nearby shoreline carefully. This is the only place to pitch camp. Everywhere else is too steep or lies beneath thin chutes that discharge a steady volley of snow, ice, and lethal rock. The goldens were planted here decades ago and forgotten. MDFWP has no record of the action, which is perfect. A sheriff with Scandinavian blood who patrolled the valley below in a battered Jeep Wagoneer told me about this water when I still had long hair (hell, any hair). He said that he carried them in a canvas bucket from a lake a couple of ridges away and dumped the trout in this lake. He did this over the period of several years and the descendants of his efforts are doing very well. Original *Oncorhynchus aguabonita* goldens from the upper South Fork of the Kern River in California's Sierra Mountains. What a long strange trip these genes have made down the years. My friend the sheriff died years ago, but his wildly colorful little trout live on and I cherish them, their history, and this diminutive piece of mountain sanity. The pusillanimous moanings of a society that slavishly practices its orthodoxy (whatever it may be this month) can be overwhelming. For me, out in the hills for even a few days means the difference between clear-eyed sanity and sinking into the depths of the mindless crowd and its corruptive cant.

The steak and the chili are "fantastic," as cousin Steve is wont to say when food tastes especially fine out in the open of the backcountry. I burned the paper plate, cleaned the silverware, chili pot, and grill, and then poured some cognac into a snifter that I also pack tightly wrapped. I know, this smacks of ostentation this far up in the mountains, but the crystal is really a nice touch. Think about it. The amber liquid swirled in the hand-warmed glass. Rich, intoxicating fumes filled the air. A Honduran cigar with an aroma of spice and roasted nuts completes this serene picture of self-indulgence. The sky is a jet black hemisphere filled with the lights of all sorts of distant objects. Shooting stars fizzle by overhead on a regular basis. Satellites pass swiftly, spying on all sorts of covert activities and mysterious weather formations. The running lights of a 727 from Kalispell to the north wink on and off in the west. The glow from the moon rises behind the Swan Range across the valley, miles distant, the peaks highlighted in dark relief in the lunar light. Almost full, the moon's bright sphere eliminates all but the brightest objects—Mars, Orion, Vega, Deneb, Polaris, Capella, the Big Dipper. The fire is excellent company, snapping and crackling to its own beat. The air smells clean, of snow. Rocks clattering downhill and splashing into the lake are the only other sounds. Sleep comes easily.

The pale light of dawn wakes me. The water bottle is empty. Frost covers the sleeping bag. Lying in the bag is the obvious play but building a fire, taking a leak, and making coffee are the wise choices. I split the difference and kill another ten minutes lying on my back watching the sky go from light blue to pink to tangerine. Sitting up I can see the goldens cruising and feeding. Do they ever rest? After coffee and a pear, I pack some fruit, cheese, oysters, and two bottles of beer in the daypack for a hike up to a saddle between two peaks. The climb crosses rock slabs layered with bands the color of dried blood. Mica and quartz sparkle in the light. Then up a grassy slope that grows steeper near the summit. The scramble takes an hour. I've not been up here in years. The view is as stunning as ever. Snow and glacier-covered mountains tower above, a series of turquoise lakes stretches out of sight along a dogleg valley of pine and meadow. Small icebergs float on their surfaces. Rivers of silver brilliance shoot out from large tunnels carved in the ice. The water falls forever, turning to spray then fine rainbow mist by the time it touches ground. Flathead Lake shimmers and low hills roll off in the west.

Normally leery of heights (to put things mildly), I dangled my feet over the edge of the saddle. The valley floor is over a thousand feet below. Small pines cling to tenuous holds in the sheer rock. This is the only exposed place that I have no fear of. Don't ask me why. I lean over and wonder what falling through the air, spinning end over end, and then crashing on the rocks below would be like. Would I experience a terror that lasts for eternity? Would I black out in shock? Or would my mind snap, gleefully embracing insanity like a long lost friend? I'd find out some other time. I ate the food I'd packed and drank the beer before leaning against a wind-battered fir and nodding off.

The romp back down to camp was easy as I "skiied" the grassy slope in my tennis shoes and hopped from boulder to boulder letting gravity and momentum do all the work. The day was warm by now, almost seventy up here. I stripped and jumped into the lake. My heart exploded. God was it cold. After paddling about a bit like a spastic springer spaniel, I climbed out and let the sun dry me. Fresh clothes felt like velvet.

The goldens eventually overcame their shock at the intrusion and returned to the area. I caught three for dinner. Each a twelve-inch clone of the other. Their stomachs were filled with midge larvae and winged adults. What they saw in the Woolly Worms I'll never know. Butter, a splash of wine, and some pepper were all that was required for the trout. I had a few cocktails, cooked the goldens, and poured some wine in the snifter. I'd left the wine glass behind. Life can be vicious at times. The goldens tasted like brook trout with a hint of the rock and snow of their environment, a very subtle flavor that went well with sliced pears. After the meal I built up the fire, leaned back against my pack, and sipped cognac into the night.

The load was much lighter coming down and I made the trip out in just over two hours, if the hour spent catching wild cutthroat in a lake along the way was subtracted. This was exactly what I wanted the trip to be. Time alone filled with emptiness, fish, mountains, and my own thoughts.

Looking back up to where I had just been, I thought that this was the right way to end another year's time in the high country. Unfortunately, it was one less year to experience, but one more to remember fondly, with feeling.

Autumn is a time when fishing for good-sized brown trout is easy in a satisfying way. The trout are in expected locations and they respond to appropriate patterns. From late September until sometime in the sleet and blustery gloom of November, brown trout are aggressive, colorful predators charged with the excitement of spawning urge. This is a time when my home state of Montana along with much of the West is dominated by the feeling that winter is holding just over the northern horizon. The smell of snow is in the air mixed with the decay of needles and leaves.

Wading favorite streams takes on an intensity that would not seem possible in the long, dry days of July and August. Even the light is different, clear like delicate crystal with an orange-gold cast. Cottonwoods blaze yellow. Larch are on fire. Undergrowth pulses with purple, red, dusky brown, and the final vestiges of summer green. The weather has turned. Crisp mornings are filled with frost and the sky when not boiling with dark storm clouds is blue—plain, pure blue. Maybe by afternoon there is a warm breeze and the nights are filled with stars, bright planets, and a silver-white moon. Even without trout I would be standing in a river, but the autumn browns empower the landscape, transforming streams and the surrounding country into classic fly fishing settings. There is no finer time of the season.

Darkness comes early in October, around seven, and at dusk in this small river browns fed steadily on *Baetis* duns just below a short riffle on the outer edge of a spinning eddy. Casting a Blue-Winged Olive with a two-weight was perfect. There was enough metallic light on the water to see both the pattern and the rise. The browns were eager and the long, light leader did not scare them. The first trout at the end of the pod was fourteen inches, bright and marked with jet black and crimson spots. Flanks and belly were copper shading to soft gold. The back was brown. Neglecting minor differences in size, all of the fish were identical—colorful, muscular, eager to hit the small dry.

By dark I'd had enough, for a few hours, and went back to camp for a drink and a grilled Rock Cornish game hen seasoned with pepper, sage, and lime juice. The river was placid where I sat and the sound of feeding browns mixed nicely with the sputterings of a small fire. Shooting stars, familiar companions on October brown trout excursions, shot overhead with regularity.

Autumn, brown trout, good weather. Perfect. None of the fish exceeded seventeen inches. The large browns would come later with overcast windblown days filled with icy rain. Then the bigger fish would cast aside their innate sense of caution and move out to eat as aggressively as their smaller relations had done this evening. By the time the browns are actively moving streambed gravels around to make redds, I move off and work to other trout or wander coulees, bluffs, and prairies looking for sharptails and huns and pheasants. Spawning is stressful for the browns, and my intrusions would only add to the strain.

The smallest streams both east and west of the Continental Divide often hold some of the largest trout. I was recently shown one that flows easily between brushy undercut banks somewhere between Helena and Missoula by a friend who shares my devotion to browns and close-quarter streams. In the summer, caddis are everything when cast sidearm beneath the overhanging limbs. Browns from eight inches to more than twenty rise eagerly and then try and run for cover in the dark water beneath the leaves and limbs. By autumn, a fall caddis with an orange body and light elk hair wing produces similar results. Working upstream, I cast to the slightest indentation in the streambed or the smallest coves in the brush, and the browns are there as they are in most streams like this in the West. Upwelling springs and marble-sized gravels are ideal habitat for invertebrates and for incubating trout eggs and then sheltering fry.

Taking the browns on dries is addicting, but working a #6 or #8 unweighted Woolly Bugger with a four-weight is entertaining, too. The cast must still be bank-tight, often skipped beneath cover, and even a stout 1X or 2X tippet snaps against the resistance of a willow branch on occasion. Quick strips catch the attention of browns that come slashing and splashing after the streamer. I've taken browns in creeks and tributaries like this from one end of the state to the other, as well as in Idaho and Wyoming. Each stream is the same but with a distinct personality and an endless variety of holding water. If you can take fish on one stream, you will do so on the others, but the experience will be different on each every time you cast.

Except for the northwestern corner of Montana in the Flathead and Kootenai drainages, every major river in the state has at least a marginal fall run of browns. All of them can be waded and will provide some action, though on certain streams floating, especially when casting streamers, makes it easier to cover and make realistic presentations.

I prefer wading a river most of the time, using streamers to take sizeable browns throughout the day, even on bright, bluebird outings. Looking for the same holds I work on the small streams, I cast to eddies, undercuts, and pockets. The major difference between a big river and a creek is size. Habitat is habitat. As long as food, shelter, and cold, oxygen-rich water are present, there will be browns and perhaps rainbow, cutthroat, and brook trout. There will always be mountain whitefish. The ubiquitous native outnumbers its more popular relations by ratios of three or four or even eight to one in this country. They play tag with the tails of streamers, tugging slightly as the pattern is wriggled through the wa-

ter. The undulating motion appeals to their better nature, but the size of the offering is beyond their means.
When the Olives are rising, whitefish are a nuisance. The
few times they fail to put down the browns, they manage
to outcompete the trout for the fly. There have been
times when I've had to sort my way through a half dozen
whitefish for every brown. Steady action, but whitefish
do not excite me.

On a small stream a sink-tip line is not required.
As the flow increases the sink-tip lines come into play. I
start with a five-foot tip and work my way up to a ten if
necessary, sometimes even adding a small split shot or
two to help sink an already heavily weighted streamer.
You can fish lighter or even dry but drifting patterns over
the head of big fish is not my idea of a good time. Adjust-
ing the system to fit the water conditions is part of the
routine. An eight-weight on a big river makes more sense
than trying to be a "sport" with a five. Digging sink-tip
line and heavy Muddlers out of strong current is work
that can eventually stress a light rod to the breaking
point. And to be fair to a hefty brown, you need a rod that
matches the fish and the current, to be able to play the
trout without overly exerting it.

One of the worst fishing days of my life was in
October when I tried to swim a weighted Bitch Creek in a
river packed with eager browns over near West
Yellowstone. Casting was impossibly dangerous, fighting
two-pound browns in fast chutes was a joke, filled with
the maddening sounds of popping tippets. I used to think
that fishing with a rod one size too small was better than
working with a stick one size too large. I know better
now. Fall browns frequently hold down deep in rough

cover. The ability to cast a clumsy setup with ease and authority is a blessing, notably in the last hours of a long, trout-filled day when the arm begins to flag a bit from the exertion.

When I hit the road for brown trout in September or October, aside from the opulence of camp life and dining I maintain, the fishing equipment list is simple: A four-weight rod with weight-forward line for streams of twenty to forty feet wide and a fast, stiff seven-weight for big rivers with a weight-forward floating line and the five- and ten-foot sink-tips. I might add a two-weight for a favorite piece of small water. But that's the extent of the rods. Because I'm a creature of bad but constant habits I always pack a box of attractor dries—Wulffs, Humpies, Trudes, and the like. I also bring fall Elk Hair Caddis and BWO imitations, plenty of tippet material, and some floatant. For the serious work, I pack a Bugger box filled with weighted and unweighted streamers from #2 to #8 in olive, black, and brown. There is also a box of Bitch Creeks, Girdle Bugs, Prince Nymphs, Marabou Muddlers (especially in yellow), Sculpins, and Zonkers. They all attract brown trout; I just happen to be inculcated with the power of Buggers. Throw in a small container of Hare's Ears, Antron Emergers, and Pheasant Tails and I'm set.

The importance of keeping the fishing gear simple is clear, considering the fact that the back of the truck is filled with chairs, a tent, sleeping bag and foam pad, cook kit, axe, saw, several coolers filled with beer, exotic coffee, cheeses, a variety of meats, eggs, vegetables, mixes, assorted crates of dry goods, and perhaps a dram of bourbon. Wading shoes, hip boots, and chest waders along with cold and wet weather clothing complete the spartan list (except for the humidor stuffed with imported cigars that rides up front with me).

The anticipation of working to large brown trout leads to a major mistake on my part, one that I repeat all too often. In my haste to catch, see, and hold a brown I often plunge into a stream without spending a few minutes taking in the situation. On one little creek in rattlesnake country outside of Roberts there are some nice trout, but I didn't see them the first few times I visited the water. I assumed that the nine- and ten-inch browns rising to the *Baetis* were the top-of-the-line fish in the ten-foot-wide stream. I'd wade and stalk these browns carefully and, I thought, quite skillfully with a #20 BWO. Catching the fish was easy and I was happy until I saw a rancher walking down the road with some browns in the eighteen-inch range. The fish had succumbed to worms, but they were a different class of trout than I'd been playing with.

It was a shocking revelation, and when I finished several minutes of circling the truck, I rigged up a small olive Woolly Bugger and hammered the water with quartering upstream casts. The results were amazing. Fat browns came from beneath the cover and raised hell with the streamer. For every trout I landed and released, I broke off four in the narrow confines of the stream. In a clear patch of bank that was sheltered by a clump of dead brown grass, I poked my rod beneath the overhang. Allowing for bend from the current, there was six or seven feet of shelter back there. The larger fish I was turning were probably the runts of this subterranean lot. Fly fishing and humbling revelations go hand in hand in the western world.

I'm afraid my addiction to fall brown trout hunting will never be satisfied if I am to maintain any domestic tranquility. Every little willow-choked creek, ditch, or canal lying out there has the potential to hold nice trout. As long as there is shelter, a source for cold water, and an absence of sediment, there will be bugs—caddis, mayflies, stoneflies, midges—in adequate numbers to feed the browns.

Something about this habitat intrigues me to madness. A little stream running within a hundred yards of a tavern in Bynum (I'd stopped in for a cheeseburger) is a case in point. I figured I'd be back home in Whitefish in well under three hours until the bartender mentioned that the guy at the end of the bar had caught a five-pound brown in a nearby creek only this morning. I was in big trouble. Receiving permission to fish the private land and gathering some directions to the best "holes," I wandered in a predatory daze through a field of volunteer wheat stubble to a stream that had all the signs of brown trout frenzy—willows, thick grass, and earthen banks along with icy water running over clean gravel. So much for the home fires.

Stepping quietly into the stream, I launched a Bugger (no surface activity sighted) tight to a curve in the stream course. One strip and a brown swirled. I watched, almost as a dispassionate observer, while the rod bent double in my hands, the tip bobbing spasmodically up and down as the strong trout tore line in spurts from the reel. The brown came to net, fat, colorful like all autumn browns, with a pronounced kype. Rows of sharp teeth cut the top of my index finger as I twisted the hook free. The fish sank from sight and scarlet blood dripped into the water. A handful of silvery-blue *Baetis* drifted by.

I'd better call home to say I'd be delayed, I thought. I hoped the landowners would let me camp beneath the small bench I dropped off of on my way in here. This looked like a two-day engagement, at least.

Two days turned out to be the right length stay— long enough to discover and partially learn the new water, but not long enough to become boring. I broke camp early the second day, deciding to head down to Talia's on the Bitterroot. There was no traffic to speak of on the roads. I blasted past Augusta and Bowmans Corner and over Rogers Pass where I dodged huge earth-moving equipment hell bent on tearing up the highway and surrounding countryside. Then it was on through Lincoln and along the upper Blackfoot River, beautiful water that forced me to pull over for a few casts. The four-weight was still rigged complete with an Elk Hair. I didn't bother with waders, opting to cast from low cutbanks and from along wide gravel banks. There were browns working in the pools and runs. Moving upstream I managed to take one or two from each holding area. The fish were in high color prior to spawning, their bellies almost copper, flanks burnished gold, and the spots bright red. An hour passed in seconds and the movement of the sun overhead said I'd better get back on the road. At Ovando I made an obligatory stop at Trixi's Saloon for a cheeseburger, fries, and a long-neck Ranier. In another hour I was fighting the traffic in Missoula, wasting ten minutes waiting for the lights at Malfunction Junction on the south side. I was glad to leave the town now turned smog-choked city. The place still had spirit and guts but had been overrun by Yuppies. It had grown too fast for its own good. Ugly split-levels covered the surrounding hills and strip development crowded the main roads. Past Lolo the country improved. I soon turned onto the lodge road. Talia was waiting. I'd called earlier. His Avon raft was loaded. We were ready to go. I tossed waders, rod, vest, and beer in the raft and we motored several miles up-stream for an easy float back down to the lodge. This eliminated the time-consuming task of setting up a shuttle—driving two rigs down to take-out, leaving one, then driving to put-in at the end of the float. The last step of retrieving the first rig was still necessary but there was a good bar in Darby.

The weather was ideal, in the sixties, sunny with puffy white cumulus clouds and a slight breeze. I fished the first stretch taking browns, cutthroat, and rainbows on the Elk Hair. It was enjoyable casting with short casts tight to banks and downed logs or just above small buck-ets where seams of current spilled, places that always held good trout. Talia worked a Bugger on his shift and tagged a couple of eighteen-inch browns and a larger rainbow. We stopped to fish below a wooden weir, paus-ing to drink beer, talk a little, and soak up the day, no doubt one of the last good ones of the season. The float was over too quickly as the lodge came into view on our left. We loaded the raft, stored our gear, and went off for the other rig and a cocktail or two.

Later, we cooked chicken on the massive grill constructed of stone from the river. We talked late into the night, already making plans for another February meeting and some possible explorations beginning in late April. Not much for goodbyes, we parted quickly the following morning. The drive back up to Whitefish was a bit melancholy, but some leaping browns on a Flathead Reservation stream put a smile on my glum visage. Rooting around in the nearly empty cooler I turned up a bottle of inexpensive Taylor champagne and toasted a memorable running of the autumn browns.

"Here's to you, damnit, and here's to next fall. May we all have many more."

There is a small lake at the base of timbered mountains near home that comes into its own for a brief period late in October. Perhaps twenty acres and not very deep, the place holds brook trout in abundance, some over five pounds. Formerly the home of beavers and fed by several tiny creeks tumbling in from the surrounding hills, the water is checked by an old cement dam that is chipped and crumbling. Many years ago the spot was the scene of Sunday picnics for Whitefish residents. Today the water plays host to occasional loads of teenagers exploring the wonders of beer, wine, sex, and other delights. A few of us older types come here to fish for the trout, longing for the exploratory days of youth.

You can take the brookies throughout the year, but the fishing is slow, often nonexistent until the sun drops over the tree line in the west. Then the fish start to feed and they will sip caddis dries and pupae imitations, or in rare moments of carelessness, they will strike gaudy, flashing streamers. But for most of the time the

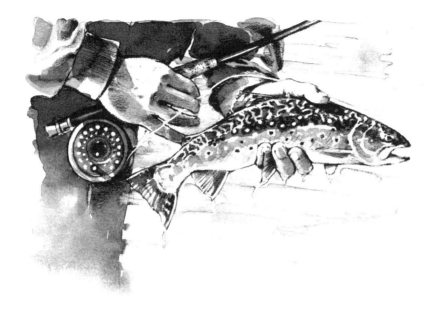

fish hide down deep or beneath jumbles of bleached, rotting logs covered with thick mats of moss and clumps of grass. A few will be seen feeding on the surface or cavorting about near shore, but they are tough to catch.

By October the brook trout are in full spawning colors, bright like the neon displays of the casinos in Whitefish, only far more desirable as a form of diversion. They swim in vast schools or band together in redd-building platoons. Large females of over twenty inches hold still near the bottom of the sidelines, watching, waiting to move onto the cleaned gravel. At these times the trout are extremely susceptible to my efforts with Flash-A-Buggers, Mickey Finns, or Copper Zonkers. They are also easily stressed. So I allow myself one day each October, no more, to fish for these brilliant fish—a few hours when I fish greedily and then, satiated, sit back in the small one-man canoe and watch the trout go about their business. Four or five small males are kept for a ritual meal with my family that evening. I don't keep many trout during a season, but the ones that are kept for the plate are savored. They make the fishing through-out the year special. Fishing without the restrained will-ingness to kill for the table is sterile, without purpose for me. I feel absolutely no need to justify the taking of these fish to anyone.

A couple of Octobers back, Steve flew out unex-pectedly from his home in Minnesota with a few friends. I brought them here. One of our number was from Sweden and had extolled the virtues of the native char in his country, admittedly a fine salmonid. After taking a couple of plump brookies, he turned to me and said, "These are very nice fish, John," and his wide-open smile said it all. We cooked several over a small fire, balancing the trout on forked willow sticks. They fell into the ashes but still tasted wild and sweet. That was one of those honest, simple days that turns special in the mind over the years mainly because of the ease with which it hap-pened. No great plans. No bullshit. Just four guys eating something they'd just caught, killed, and cooked.

I've been doing this for several seasons now, tracking the best time in my fishing logs. I know the peak day, give or take a couple. Too early and the trout spook at the canoe's shadow, darting and dodging madly for shelter. Too late and the fish are spawned out, tired. They need to spend the long winter recuperating.

Each year the way into the lake grows worse with erosion, which is fine with me. The harder it is to come in here, the better. The ground is covered with cottonwood and willow leaves. The larch are bright orange, their reflections blazing on the smooth surface of the lake. The temperature is near forty and there are high clouds. Mallards water-walk into the sky at my approach. I take my time rigging up and loading the canoe before placing the entire works in the water. (One year I forgot the paddle and was forced to use a long, wide piece of bark from the cottonwoods.) After turning and twisting and rocking over a number of partially submerged logs, I break free out into the open water. Following the dark vein of an old stream takes me to a sheltered bay filled with laboring trout. Redds are being built all around, the sites blue-white next to the surrounding brown silt and detritus. Males from eight to over twenty inches are cruising everywhere, singly and in groups of as many as a dozen. Their humped backs and well-defined kypes are easy to see through three feet of perfectly clear water.

I cast the Bugger beyond a redd, perhaps an effort of thirty feet with the two-weight. The pattern sinks to the bottom in seconds. Some trout turn to watch. They close in as it approaches the redd. Then three fish pounce on the fly as it crosses an invisible boundary near the spawning site. I lift the rod at the attack and a brook trout with an orange belly so bright it glows tears up the surface before coming quickly to net. The fish is a riot of color—sky blue, emerald, black, white, scarlet, pink, purple, yellow. I think that they really are more spectacular than goldens. It is just over a foot, much smaller than several other males nearby, so I whack its head on the gunnel. The brook quivers then goes still. I lift the lid of the wicker creel and place it in some moist yellow-green ferns I'd plucked earlier. I decide to catch one of roughly the same size for each member of my family, a total of five.

This is not as easy as it first appears. The larger males, trout over fifteen inches, are quicker and more aggressive. I sift through a number of them to find four more of proper length. In between I release trout up to nearly twenty inches, taking fish on almost every cast. The reason I only come here once a year is obvious. I could never restrain myself from casting to these trout. I could never come and just watch. I'm still too much the predator to be satisfied by voyeurism.

Beneath a couple of logs I spot several smaller males near another redd. On the first cast the fly sticks to one of the deadfalls and the fish scatter when I pull my canoe over, using the line, and remove the fly. The trout return within minutes and the next cast hits wood, bouncing into the water and drifting toward bottom. The pattern never reaches its goal. A huge fish comes from nowhere and slams into the Bugger. I raise the rod instinctively and the trout turns for cover, then switches course and streaks for the other end of the lake. Line whizzes off the small reel, the drag makes a hell of a racket, and the trout hits the backing—the first time for that here. Reeling in line turns the shallow-draft canoe and the craft begins to slip ever so slowly toward the stubborn fish. I can propel the twelve-foot boat with my hand, it's true, but the fact that the brook trout is of sufficient heft to influence the canoe is amazing. The trout runs twice more and then comes steadily to me. The fish is enormous and will not fit in the net. Exhausted, it rests on its side next to me. I mark the length against the rod in the water.

This is one of those fish that is very difficult to turn loose. The atavism within boils in my stomach, rushes up my chest, and tingles down into my fingers. I almost yield to the urge to kill the trout, almost. Then the feeling subsides and the hook is twisted from the corner of the curved jaw. The brook, perhaps sensing this brush with death, snaps to and disappears with splashing pumps of its tail.

"Well, that sure as hell made my day," I say out loud to the trees. Hands shaking, I measure the mark on the rod. Twenty-two inches. I drift toward the other brook trout and take a small one on the next cast. That's all. I've had enough. What dependable, special water. As reliable as natural clockwork. Every year the little lake rattles my nerves this way. One day is plenty. Any more would reek of greed. Just give me the one day.

A storm has come up suddenly, and the sky has lowered with dark, charcoal clouds that boil and churn not far above. Small spikes of angry moisture looking like miniature tornadoes shoot out at odd angles, then vanish in spinning mist. Snow razors down in sheets, slapping my face, hissing as it crashes into the lake. A puff of snow whirls around my neck and shoulders, cold, icy. I shiver. Time for home. The scent of winter is strong on the wind. This year's fishing is almost done.

This is ridiculous, a bad habit turned into raving addiction. No twelve-step program can help with a vice gone this far around the bend. Less than a week from

Thanksgiving, a foot of snow on the ground, temperatures below thirty, and there is ice lining the sides of the riverbed. Ideal conditions. For what, though? A frigid, watery suicide? A frostbite competition? Surely not fly fishing.

Several sunny days linked together did the trick. I had to go fishing so now I was standing in the Flathead River not far from the confluence of the Middle and North forks in water close to the top of my hip waders. Long underwear, wool shirt, sweater, waxed cotton coat, wool hat, and mittens, yes this was fly fishing and nothing could be finer. An eight-weight rod was coupled with a seven-weight sink-tip, strong leader, and an ugly streamer. Real ugly—long white marabou tail, bright green floss covering thirty wraps of fuse wire, and bushy, soft badger hackle all gracefully piled on a #2 4X-long hook. The quarry was lake trout, an introduced species that was wiping out the native bull trout. The MDFWP said this was only one of several reasons for the decline, but the bull trout were holding their own in the Swan River and the only difference between it and the Flathead drainage was that a power company had built a dam near the mouth of the Swan that blocked the upstream movement of the lake trout. The species has recently been documented in the British Columbia section of the North Fork. How to rid the system of the lake trout was anybody's guess, and eventually unchecked clear-cutting and development would finish off even the Swan's population of bulls. The streamer I was flinging far out in the current was designed to imitate immature bulls and other forage fish.

I arrived around 9:15 a.m., just as the sun burned through some morning fog. The first cast, about seventy-five feet with a couple of upstream mends and then sufficient line stripping to absorb the slack, went fishless. The second cast closer in drifted through the run and then swung in toward the bouldery shore sliding over a rocky shelf. A large fish boiled on the surface as it smacked the pattern. The rod bent double and line was pulled steadily from the reel. The charge stopped after a hundred feet and I began to pump and wind the trout into the calm water I was stumbling about in. Two casts and a lake trout. Not bad. I walked the fish up the bank. Thirty inches and close to ten pounds. Dinner would be broiled Mackinaw steaks and drawn butter. I was on a one-man mission, a futile crusade of sorts, to rid the river of lake trout. They were killing the bulls. Perhaps if

I could catch say fifty or sixty thousand in the next few days things would shift in favor of the natives. The goal seemed realistic to me, plus offering a wonderful excuse to go fishing.

I gutted the fish. The stomach was jammed with eight-inch bull trout in the early stages of digestion. All the markings were visible. No wonder the bulls were disappearing. Another hour of vengeful casting turned three more lake trout from eighteen inches to twenty-nine, all full of juvenile bulls.

Enforcing the closure of the bull trout season was going to be a nightmare. The two fish feed on similar prey in similar locations during similar times of the day. To those not familiar with both species, it would be easy to confuse the two. They both have wide, flattened skulls, thick silvery-olive drab bodies (at this time of year), and pale markings—orange spotting for the bulls and lighter slashes for the lake trout. I've seen a number of anglers bragging about the giant bull trout they'd caught when it was really a lake trout, or commenting on the bright colors of a laker that was actually a spawning bull trout. One of the few significant behavioral differences is the fact that lake trout do not build redds. Bulls do.

To be honest, this was fun. Catching a thirty-inch fish in the ten-pound range on a fly rod in Montana or anywhere else is not all that common. Maybe in Alaska or the Northwest Territories or possibly Siberia or Mongolia, but not in the West. And to be doing this in late November was an added kick. There was also the possibility of tying into a bull trout (by accident, of course), or a large Lake Superior whitefish (another bull trout predatorial curse), or even a sleek rainbow or cutthroat trout. I'd seen several leaping after emerging caddis already, including a few almost at my feet.

By 10:30 the fishing had stopped. The light was too intense and the feeding lanes were too exposed for the fish. I lugged twenty-five pounds of lake trout up to the truck and dropped the load in the bed filled with snow from the night before. Maybe I'd smoke a couple for snacks. A bottle of Finlandia was chilling in a snowbank. I launched a maduro cigar of Mexican heritage with a sulphur-spitting stick match of obviously poor lineage and poured a healthy blast of vodka into a small glass I'd brought for the occasion. The liquor was cold fire and the cigar tasted full-bodied, rich. The river rushed past. Mist hung in thick bands in the forested hills. Leaning forward I could see far up both the North and Middle forks and well down the main river and its tall banks of sand and gravel. More vodka and another puff on the cigar. This was indeed nice fishing in scenic surroundings. It was too bad the lake trout came at the expense of the bulls. I wished this weren't so and drained the glass. Tomorrow I'd rise well before sunrise and be fishing before dawn.

The next morning I was standing in the water surrounded by darkness. The roiled surface of the river reflected the slight ambient light in silvery braids that rippled and twisted in patterns of infinite variation. The marks of my wading yesterday, the footprints in gravel and rock cleaned of loose debris, were barely visible now that my eyes had adjusted to the gloom. The line whistled back and forth in the air well to my right side in case the ungainly streamer had ideas of drawing blood from my scalp or perhaps picking off an ear. I launched the fly upstream and mended line, replicating casts made when I could see what I was doing. About when I guessed that the line and pattern were brushing the streambed, I stripped in line erratically, mimicking a wounded or frightened fish. Almost immediately, above the shelf this time, something slammed the fly and the rod jerked and bobbed as line ran off the reel. I felt my way cautiously backwards through the water to shore and the fish followed thrashing the surface with its head, gills flared, all of this faintly seen in the first blue hints of dawn. The lake trout flopped madly when it felt the cold stab of the dry rocks on its flanks. Dropping the rod, I covered the fish with my chest and arms and tried to subdue it with my hands. This one was thirty inches, I guessed, as I took it to the truck and dropped it in the snow still smeared with blood from the first outing's trout.

I took two more in thirty minutes and missed several strikes. By daylight the fishing shut down. I walked up and down the river casting to likely looking holds and runs and scared up a rainbow of a couple of pounds. The fishing now was more out of habit, routine. Another twenty pounds of lake trout. My family would soon hate fish, but the mission was not complete. I still had between 49,993 and 59,993 lake trout to go in my bull trout rescue mission. I'd be back tomorrow.

Several dark mornings later the fishing had gone south. Either all of the fish in this run had been caught by me (most unlikely) or they'd moved back downstream into Flathead Lake. The days were colder now and every couple of casts the guides had to be cleared of ice. The line was an old beater. Why ruin a good one on the jagged stuff? The fishing for me this season was over. I'd had enough for awhile. Over 150 days and a lot of water. Time to write, enjoy the holidays, and think of other things beside fly fishing.

Walking up to the truck, my image in the cab window was startling. Almost gaunt, in need of a shave, eyes slightly bulged, I was reminded of E. Annie Proulx's superb short story, "The Wer-Trout," dealing with obsession, guilt, conscience, and madness, "In the shining curve of glass he sees his reflection; the chinless throat, the pale snout, the vacant rusted eyes of the Wer-Trout."

I wasn't afraid in the least. Perhaps it was the Jack Daniels before dinner and the wine with dinner, but I definitely was not afraid. As each slide was projected on the screen the appropriate and apparently entertaining words poured from my mouth. The shots of large goldens, bulls, brooks, cutthroat, and rainbows drew sighs and groans from the audience. How I wound up in Boston in December at the monthly meeting of the Boston Fly Casters is a mystery to me. I remember the group's entertainment coordinator, George Ticknor, calling in the spring and asking if I would do a presentation. I said "No!" I'd never done such a thing before and really had no plans to do any in the future. Perhaps they teach subliminal persuasion at Harvard. At any rate I wound up agreeing to the engagement plus a shorter show at the Boston Orvis store the night before. In addition to making some money, George kindly routed my return trip through Albany, allowing me the opportunity to visit Bob Jones and his wife, Louise, at their home in Vermont. I almost didn't make it that far, but that part comes later.

Loud applause marked the end of the show. They were a generous bunch. Back at the table I asked one of the members, a psychiatrist, if he thought I was doing all right. He replied "You're doing better than I am." Should this statement have worried me? I don't know. After the show we went for drinks and the next day I went to Logan to catch my flight. Fat chance. A once-every-hundred-years storm, a late-season hurricane, closed the airport for that day and the next as it turned out. George graciously offered to put me up at his house, again. His wife, Kathy, a new mother, recovered her composure quickly when she saw me unexpectedly at the door. George came home from work, mixed some of his justifiably famous martinis (Boodles gin), which we polished off with dispatch before heading out to rent a couple of videos. After his wife and young son, Ben, went off to bed, we started in on a large bottle of Johnny Walker Black. Conversation centered on fishing and the only things I remember are parts of *The Texas Chainsaw Massacre* (the scene where the guy jumps up from the freezer) and some music by a seductive group called the Cowboy Junkies. One of those nights.

George was slow off the mark the next day, so Kathy introduced me to her neighbors (some of this should be coming clear by now). Two feet of snow had fallen that night. No one was moving. The neighbor and I talked about turkey hunting, inventing, and the beginnings of the Revolutionary War, which in turn led to his giving me a tour of Concord complete with his unique version of how the war really started. Suffice it to say that sex, drunkenness, and gun play were involved, and I soon found myself sitting in the Concord Inn drinking beer in the very room where the boys had retired after that blast over two-hundred years ago. Later we shoveled George's and the neighbor's walks while drinking blackberry brandy. By flight time the next day I was a bit tired.

Bob met me at the airport in Albany, New York, and we drove into Vermont. Small creeks, springs, rivers, and ponds were everywhere. Gorgeous water. Fine country. I wished it were late spring so that I could work rivers like the Mettowee and the Battenkill. Louise cooked wonderful meals during my stay—homemade breads and soups, leg of lamb, baked steelhead. Bob and I stayed up late into the nights talking writing, fishing, hunting, Africa, local history. Dogs and cats were everywhere as they should be in a home. I felt at ease. We even managed to crawl out and go hunting for ruffed grouse one sunny afternoon. No birds, but that was not important. Bob's golden lab, Jake, proved to be one of the most energetic, powerful workers I'd ever seen afield. Louise's Jack Russell, Ros, was equally impressive in a more down-to-earth way. Both fine hounds. I was sorry to leave, but Christmas was near and I missed the family.

So what does all of this have to do with fishing, you ask? Nothing and everything.

The joy, the magic of fly fishing is the unexpected, the intriguing, the beautiful, and the flat out strange. Twenty years ago I never would have believed that I would be making a living from writing about this passion of mine, that I would be flying to the East Coast to talk about trout or walking grouse coverts in Vermont. The friends I've made on the water are as good as any man could want. People like Bob, Talia, Tony, and so many others. They alone would justify the time spent casting to fish.

Then there is the country—the mountains, rivers, deserts, out-of-the-way towns, the animals, the forests. Put aside the fact that connecting with a wild trout taps into some primitive instinct that harks back to our days as hunter-gatherers or the visceral pleasure of catching fish; time spent in these surroundings is in itself ample inducement to pile into the truck and head down the road. There is an aura of craziness that swirls around fly fishing, an intoxicating sense that something unique, bizarre, and unexpected is waiting for me only a few feet upstream or in the next bay. I chase this natural drug with all my heart every chance I get. That's all there really is to this hopeless addiction. It's all really quite simple, as it should be.

But right now I've got to sort some slides of brook trout for an article I'm working on.

Damn, those are nice brookies. I bet that lake is frozen solid enough to stand on. An axe, a short rod, the snowshoes, and a Thermos of brandied hot chocolate.

The hell with the article. Better bring the four-weight. There might be open water, maybe some late *Baetis* coming off.

I'm out of here...

Other titles by
COUNTRYSPORT, INC.

Dreaming the Lion: Reflections on Hunting, Fishing, and a Search for the Wild
by *Thomas McIntyre*

A Breed Apart: A Tribute to the Hunting Dogs that Own Our Souls, Volumes I & II

A.H. Fox: The Finest Gun in the World by *Michael McIntosh*

Bare November Days: A Tribute to Ruffed Grouse

Birds on the Horizon: Wingshooting Adventures Around the World
by *Stuart Williams*

The Countrysport Wingshooter's Journal: A Bird Hunter's Personal Diary

Best Guns by *Michael McIntosh*

The Big-Bore Rifle: The Book of Fine Magazine & Double Rifles .375 - .700 Calibers
by *Michael McIntosh*

Call of the Quail: A Tribute to the Gentleman Game Bird

Come October: Exclusively Woodcock

Eastern Upland Shooting by *Dr. Charles C. Norris*

Robert Churchill's Game Shooting: The Definitive Book on the Churchill Method of
Instinctive Wingshooting and Sporting Clays by *Robert Churchill and Macdonald Hastings*

The Grand Passage: A Chronicle of North American Waterfowling

"Mr. Buck": The Autobiography of Nash Buckingham

Training Retrievers: The Cotton Pershall Method by *Bobby N. George, Jr.*

Robert Ruark's Africa by *Robert C. Ruark*

Shotgunner's Notebook: The Advice and Reflections of a Wingshooter by *Gene Hill*

The following Countrysport Press titles are also available in DELUXE LIMITED EDITIONS:
Chasing Fish Tales: A Freewheeling Year in the Life of an Angler

Dreaming the Lion: Reflections on Hunting, Fishing, and a Search for the Wild

A Breed Apart: A Tribute to the Hunting Dogs that Own Our Souls, Volumes I & II

Bare November Days: A Tribute to Ruffed Grouse

Birds on the Horizon: Wingshooting Adventures Around the World

The Big-Bore Rifle: The Book of Fine Magazine & Double Rifles .375 – .700 Calibers

Eastern Upland Shooting

The Grand Passage: A Chronicle of North American Waterfowling

"Mr. Buck": The Autobiography of Nash Buckingham

The Countrysport Deluxe Limited Editions feature:
- *deluxe leather binding*
- *gilt-edged top papers*
- *ribbon bookmark*
- *specially commissioned gold foil cover art*
- *commemorative title page bearing the edition size*

For ordering information write or call:
COUNTRYSPORT, P.O. Box 1856, Traverse City, MI 49685
1-800-367-4114